Feng Shui for Relationships

...gives you the awareness that your environment, in this case the weather, has a much greater impact on your wellbeing than any of us would like to admit. ...It is only a small step towards the awareness that everthing in nature is connected.

Feng Shui for Relationships

The Yin & Yang of Love

Shan-Tung Hsu

New Age Books

ISBN: 978-81-7822-197-7

First Indian Edition: 2009

(Reprinted from *The Yin and Yang of Love: Feng Shui for Relationships published* by Llewellyn Publications, USA)

Published by
NEW AGE BOOKS
A-44 Naraina Phase-I
New Delhi-110 028 (INDIA)
Email: nab@vsnl.in
Website: www.newagebooksindia.com

For Sale in Indian Subcontinent Only

Printed in India
at Shri Jainendra Press
A-45 Naraina Phase-I, New Delhi-110 028

To all people in love and yearning for love.

Contents

Preface

In the long period during which I've been teaching Feng Shui and providing Feng Shui consultations, I have found that one of the most frequent and important concerns people have is about their relationships.

Many of my students, as well as my clients, have been looking to Feng Shui for answers to their questions about relationships. They ask if there might be some way that Feng Shui could help them to improve an existing relationship, or to find a lover.

Their intuition is right in pointing them to Feng Shui as a factor in these difficulties. There often are space-related issues involved: the spaces in which they are living are just not adequate to nourish a loving relationship, or are even likely to create conflict. At the same time, space itself is seldom the only source of difficulties. Part of their problem also has to do with misperceptions or misunderstandings, which lead to awkward or inharmonious handling of energy.

In this book, I am trying to deal more comprehensively with the situation: not just with issues of space, but with issues of the energetics of relationships, and how the energetic factors interact with the spatial factors.

I am very aware that love and relationships are complex and delicate subjects. Throughout human history, millions of books have tried to address these issues. When I first thought of trying to write something on this subject, I realized right away that it was an ambitious task, but my students and friends kept urging me to write—and my clients' reactions to the consultations they received also encouraged me.

I decided that it would be most useful to approach the subject from the essence of Feng Shui. Feng Shui sees human activities as part of nature, and in the context of natural processes. It is a point of view that integrates human beings and nature, and also integrates nature with the whole process by which things come to be and pass away. It is a holistic and complete point of view. It encompasses all time and space—a knowledge that is "naturally" in all of us, since our relationship to the cosmos is one of similarity. In other words, the key to our relationship to the cosmos is the fact that the essential structures of the cosmos and of human existence are the same.

Feng Shui approaches spatial design from the point of view of energetic relationships. In this book I approach romantic relationships from the same kind of energetic point of view—in terms of Yin and Yang, rather than in terms of male and female. At first this perspective may seem so abstract that it loses all the detail. But I hope it will also give a more complete picture.

To present such a picture, I start with general energetic issues, and go on to talk about space and time factors. Since human beings are living, social organisms, it is also necessary to deal with communication, interpersonal energetics, food, and sexual activity. I have therefore devoted one chapter to each of these subjects. Even in these chapters, though, I have avoided getting too involved with details, and tried to link everything back to the larger energetic issues. It is this larger context that is so often missing in modern life. For many people nowadays, life is very specialized and very choppy because people spend so much of their time focused on very narrow areas of their worlds.

There are many books and workshops that deal with relationships, that try to give people techniques for improving their relationships. Some of these approaches tend to present things from a purely spiritual point of view; others present them from an intellectual point of view, or focus on emotional responses. Such approaches can inspire people for a while, but it is easy to go back to the way things were before. The problem is that whatever changes they bring about are only on the level of ideas and emotions, and do not engage the more fundamental level of formative energy. This is why it is so important to talk about the role of formative energy in romance.

In a very real sense, there are no special ideas or "secrets" to be found in this book: on an intellectual level, everything presented here is pretty much common sense, but everything in our approach aims to make changes at the level of energy, not at the level of ideas.

This is not a big book, a comprehensive book, or a complicated book—and I certainly hope it doesn't seem that way to anyone. I am not trying to come up with the last word, or a brand-new word—just some helpful words. If every reader finds a few sentences that resonate, I will feel I have hit my mark.

Acknowledgments

I am very thankful for my many students and friends who encouraged me to write this book. I would also like to thank the following people for providing careful reading and suggestions throughout the writing process: David Abbot, Bertha Aybar, Myrna Elias, Kate Fletcher, Irene Gonzalez, Christy Raedek, Bekka Rauve, Nance Scott, Barbara Setters, and Helga Umpierre.

In addition, I would like to extend thanks to Jo Rothenberg, who helped with the final stages of proofreading and editing. This book also owes much to the work of Earl King, Jr., who supported it by helping with the writing and revising.

1

Love: A Natural Thing

Human history is made by men and women, and thus it is largely a history of love—love frustrated, love fulfilled, love denied, love delayed. Whatever goes on, love has a lot to do with it. The eternal process of male-female relationship—entanglement, hope and despair, joy and sorrow—is the foundation for the creation of human history and culture, of the music, poetry, and stories that make us stand out from other living things (since, as far as we know, human beings are the only ones in our world who tell stories).

Indeed, throughout the world and throughout history, behind all differences in culture, religion, or politics, and behind the differences between city people, farmers, or nomads, there is always the presence of love, passion, and romance, which establish their own order to events. Some people even claim that all human endeavors are an attempt to fulfill (or at least deal with) the desire for love.

People often look at love as a matter of male-female relationship, and many books have focused tightly on romantic relationships. This book, however, approaches the matter from the point of view of Feng Shui, in an attempt to see it in a larger context, as well as in terms of the higher order phenomena that shape it.

Love as Nature Sees It

Nowadays, most people mistakenly see Feng Shui as simply being an art of placement—a way of arranging and designing space to bring benefits and avoid difficulties. However, what we call Feng Shui is traditionally called *Kan Yi* (the Tao of heaven and the Tao of earth), and the teachings described by that term guide us in all aspects of life in its relationship to the universal principles of heaven and earth. The fundamental principle of these teachings is to live in harmony with nature, and to follow natural law. This understanding of natural law has been summarized in the form of Yin-Yang Theory and Five Element Theory, which describe the knowledge of the static configurations and dynamic transformations that constitute the universe.

Yin-Yang Theory states that every relationship exists as a relationship between polarized qualities, which coexist and are mutually dependent. These polarized qualities nourish each other and restrain each other at the same time; they also transform into each other. A perfect relationship is based on the balanced participation of these two polarized qualities.

Everything in the universe is in continuous transformation. While Yin-Yang Theory describes static configurations, Five Element Theory describes the process of change. Five Element Theory uses the concrete images of wood, fire, earth, metal, and water to describe the five basic patterns in which transformations occur, the results of such transformations, and the relationships between these patterns of transformation. These five patterns, like Yin and Yang, are also mutually nourishing and mutually restraining. Again, an ideal relationship between these modes of transformation involves achieving a balance between nourishment and restraint.

From this point of view, love between men and women is just one of the forms taken by the relationship of Yin and Yang. Since Yin and Yang exist in everything in the universe, the Feng Shui point of view sees Yin-Yang relationships as occurring not just among human beings, or among animals, or even only among living beings, but among all entities, at every level. It is the same kind of relationship that exists between the river and the land through which it runs, the continent and the oceans that surround it, the wind and the forest through which it sings, and the butterfly and the flowers through which it wanders. These are all expressions of the interaction of the Yin and Yang energies of the universe.

Seen in this way, the roots of love and romance lie far deeper than matters of pleasure and pain, or laughter and tears. To understand love in the higher sense, we must look beyond its immediate manifestations, whether internal or external. We must see it free of superficial images of strife and entanglement, free of the webs of emotion. We tend to get stuck at the level of surface manifestations, which form the material for poetry, music, drama, and art. Most advice about relationships, most theory, most strategy and tactics focus on this level, and most human beings spend their lives indulging in never-ending entanglements with the pieces on the game-board of love, trying to move them into a pattern that comes out just the way they want it.

But love is more than two people sharing a chocolate milk shake. There is much more depth to it. It is never as simple as a mere physical action, or a pleasant, superficial pastime, or a period of intense passion. There are always complications—not just by accident, but by the very nature of love itself, which connects with some of the deepest structures of the universe. Unless we can see it from that deeper point of view, we wander endlessly in a maze of repetitions of the same relationship scripts.

At the same time, there is a difference between seeing from a higher level and dissecting from a lower level. To dissect from a lower level is to turn love into a mechanical product of some collection of parts. To see from a higher or deeper point of view, however, is to preserve the fullness of the experience, to see it in a context of even deeper and broader experience. To see from this deeper point of view, we have to be able to recognize the deep structures of the universe. And the best place to begin is with the deepest: the structure of the Tai Chi.

Tai Chi: The Very Beginning

From the point of view of Chinese metaphysics, everything in the universe is an interaction of Yin and Yang energies. The manifestation of the universe itself is a result of transformations arising from the interactions of Yin and Yang. The traditional way in which these interactions are summarized is in the familiar Tai Chi diagram (figure 1.1).

Figure 1.1: The Tai Chi symbol

This diagram encapsulates a vast amount of traditional teaching about the universe and about the laws of nature, ready to be unfolded by anyone who has the key to its interpretation. It is one representation of the concept of the Tao, or the Way of the Universe. Although many people have seen this diagram, there is a lot more to it than most people may realize. By beginning with the Tai Chi diagram and the teachings encoded within it, we can come to understand things in higher order terms.

Let's take some time to explore the meaning of this symbol more deeply. The term "Tai Chi" is composed of two terms: "Tai," meaning "great," and "Chi," meaning "extreme" or "ultimate." Thus, "Tai Chi" means something like the "great ultimate," that is, the universe, in the biggest and most encompassing sense of the term: the Whole.

Chinese metaphysics sees every part of nature as containing all the information of the whole, though in less detail, just as the DNA in any cell contains the information that unfolds to make a whole human body, or each piece of a hologram contains the whole image. On every level, each entity is complete by itself: a cell is a complete whole, as is a body, a planet, a solar system, or a galaxy. And each one as a whole mirrors the whole that is the others. It is always the same manifestation; the difference is a matter of scale. In an important sense, every entity, every interaction, every event, every phenomenon, including every kind of love relationship, can be represented by the Tai Chi diagram, which is a symbol of the Whole.

Let's take a closer look at the structure of this symbol. Why is it circular, and not some other shape, like square, or triangular? What is the meaning of the two fishlike shapes? Why is it divided by an S-shaped curve rather than a straight line? Why does the dark area have a white dot, and the light area a dark dot? And, again, why are the dots circular rather than some other shape?

The circle is the natural form: everything in the universe tends toward being circular. Physical objects, and events in time, are curving, cyclic, and tend toward being circular unless interfered with by other objects or events. And even those interferences tend toward the circular on their own level.

A circle is not a static thing, it is a process—one in which there is no beginning and no ending. At the same time, each point on a circle or event in the process is both a beginning and an ending. Even in terms of the concept of cause and effect, which seems to imply a simple, linear sequence, the effect of one cause is the cause of another effect, in unending sequence. As we begin to see things from this larger perspective, to see events as part of a cycle rather than as points on a line that goes in only one direction, our understanding of the meaning and value of these events begins to change and deepen.

The two internal fishlike shapes, one dark and one light, represent the two polarized energies that exist in everything. The light aspect is called Yang; the dark aspect is called Yin. The Yang aspect is often associated with the following characteristics: active, dynamic, aggressive, open, expansive. The Yin aspect is associated with the opposite characteristics: passive, static, yielding, closed, withdrawing. Thus, in the universe, heaven is Yang and earth is Yin; in a day, the daytime is Yang and the nighttime Yin. Among animals, the male is Yang and the female is Yin; in motion, upward is Yang and downward is Yin; in the seasons, summer is Yang and winter is Yin. Hot and cold, sweet and sour, joy and sorrow, success and failure, and so on: experience is a fabric woven of polarized possibilities.

The S-curve between the two aspects indicates the intimacy of their interaction and interconnection. Because of the S-shaped boundary, no matter how you slice the diagram in half, each half will always have some Yin and some Yang. This symbolizes the inseparability of Yin and Yang.

The light dot in the dark section and the dark dot in the light section indicate that each contains the other: in every Yang there is Yin, and in every Yin there is Yang. In every divine being there is a seed of a devil; in every devil there is a seed of a divinity. This is the basis of the dynamism of events: there is always transformation, because each thing contains seeds of its opposite, which give rise to change.

The fact that each dot is circular indicates that it too is a complete universe, within which there is also Yin and Yang. Yin and Yang cannot exist apart from each other. They limit each other, but they also enhance each other, give rise to each other, and transform into each other. And all events and all objects, at every scale, are expressions, from moment to moment, of these interactions. What is true for the realm of abstract relationships is also true for the specifics of the relationship between lovers.

But these interactions are not random processes: they are driven by a deeper desire, on the part of both aspects. That deeper desire is the desire for unity, through which the division can be resolved, and the primordial unity reestablished.

All the transformations of the universe are part of a process of seeking a unified equilibrium. The same thing is true of human relationships. What manifests as sexual desire, romance, and love is a shadow of the deeper desire of the soul to return to its original unity, to become again a complete Tai Chi, a full, balanced entity. This is the hidden purpose at work behind the relationships between men and women. Not only is human history a love story, but the whole history of the universe is a love story, and every event within it is an incident in that story.

So Now Everything Is Yin-Yang

Once we understand this, we can use the concepts of Yin and Yang to map the ways in which things transform. We can, for example, take men as expressions of Yang, and women as expressions of Yin, and see their relationship as a particular example of Yin-Yang relationship. It is important to remember, however, that Yin energy can manifest in a male body, and Yang energy in a female body. The interplay of Yin and Yang is just as present, from the higher order point of view, in a loving relationship between two men or two women as it is in a loving relationship between a man and a woman. The fact that the relationship between male and female is one manifestation of the Yin-Yang relationship does not mean that it is the only manifestation. Every kind of relationship has to involve polarity. Without polarity there is nothing to distinguish the participants. Without distinction, there is no basis for relationship; as soon as there is distinction, there is polarity. The key is to learn to look for, and to see, the polarizations that are present.

A smooth relationship is not too different from, for example, smooth waves (Yang) rolling up on a nice, sandy beach (Yin); a stormy relationship is not too different from the crashing of waves (Yang) upon jagged rocks (Yin). One of the main differences is that, from a human point of view, people make value judgments while nature does not. But the actual substance of the interaction of Yin and Yang is the same.

As human beings, we are affected by the whole universe. We are intimately affected by time and space. To understand how and why particular events manifest, we must understand the influence of these larger, universal factors. We cannot understand ourselves without understanding our particular situation in space and time.

This is where Feng Shui, as it is traditionally understood, comes into the picture. In this book we address the manifestations of polarity in the human world, and in particular in love and romantic relationships. Feng Shui is often regarded as only an art of environmental design, and because this is indeed a part of Feng Shui, we will look in detail at how specific living spaces can affect our relationships. We will talk about what kinds of energies manifest in what kinds of spaces, and how we can work with those spaces and energies to design arrangements that will nourish and support, rather than undermine, our lives and loving relationships.

However, we will also go beyond the limits of the ordinary understanding of Feng Shui to deal with other factors, like diet, exercise, communication, and sexuality, since these also can have effects on energetic patterns both within us and around us, which in turn have an effect on our love relationships. This is not outside the original, traditional understanding of Feng Shui: it is very much in tune with the traditional view of applying its principles to all aspects of life.

2

Human Beings and the Universe

From the human point of view, we are at the center of the universe. In one of the most important books of Taoism, the *Tao Teh Ching* (or *Dao De Jing*), it is said that there are four great things in the universe: the Tao, heaven, earth, and humanity. This means that human beings exist between heaven and earth, and are governed by the Tao, by the principles of nature. We are one of the major aspects of the great organic whole that constitutes existence. At the same time, we are an image of that whole—or, perhaps better, we are that whole, but on a different, more condensed, scale.

The Cosmic Pattern

Before we can talk about romance, we must begin from a higher level, by seeing human relationships in terms of the relationship between Yin and Yang.

As mentioned in chapter 1, Yin and Yang exist in every phenomenon at every level in the universe. They also exist in human beings, where males generally manifest Yang energy, and females generally manifest Yin energy. Age-old literature describes the differences—physical, emotional, and mental—between male and female. These differences are always influenced by culture, religion, race, and history, as well as by climate and geographic region. Sometimes, by focusing too specifically on the male-female level, one misses the larger and more general picture. This is why we will begin from the energy level of Yin and Yang relationship.

Many things in nature can be understood in terms of Yin and Yang: down and up, dark and light, cold and warm, and so on, but the fundamental difference is that one energy is more involved with the unmanifested or nonmanifest side of things, and the other is more involved with the manifest side of things. All other polarities derive from this.

The differences between human male and female are best understood in terms of aspects of manifest and nonmanifest traits. The manifest, or Yang, traits have to do with outward orientation and outward projection; the nonmanifest, or Yin, traits have to do with inward orientation and inner qualities. Manifestation is the norm for men; they are less sensitive to subtleties that depend on having an awareness of one's own responses. For women it is the other way around: it is often through awareness of their responses that they perceive things outside themselves. Because of this, there is a difference in sensitivity: men measure by pounds and tons; women measure by ounces and grams.

These polarities can manifest in thousands of ways in our lives, as the roles between men and women change from time to time. However, the basic dynamic structure we have described underlies all the particulars, no matter how they may happen to be arranged in any specific situation. To the extent that we can recognize and understand the difference between Yang and Yin energies, we can begin to see how they manifest in all possible ways in the interactions between male and female.

The existence of this difference is vitally important. It is only because of this polarity that there is a drive for interaction. Without distinction or difference there cannot be polarity; without polarity, there is no flow of energy.

Neither Yin nor Yang energy can fulfill itself: each needs its counterpart. Without its counterpart, there can be no transcendence. This is why difference and distinction can be a positive, rather than a negative, feature of existence. When we can recognize and follow the distinction and interplay between Yin and Yang on the more obvious levels of male and female, we will become more adept at recognizing the more subtle combinations and interchanges between Yin and Yang in more complex situations.

The Human Drama

If the world is a stage, and life is a drama, then all human history is a play with millions of characters. Among all these characters, however, there are ultimately only two roles: male and female. The natural difference between men and women can be traced back to the fundamental difference between Yin and Yang and their associated qualities. Males manifest more Yang energy; females manifest more Yin energy.

In order to begin to see how this interaction works, it is useful to look at certain standard or conventional contrasts between Yang and Yin as they often play out in differences between males and females. It is important to remember that these contrasts are highly simplified for the purpose of getting a handle on the nature of the differences involved. The contrasts are almost stereotypes—but this is because they represent very general averages or summaries of a wide range of actual manifestations. They are useful just the way an average is useful: they give some idea of where the center of the range of possibilities lies. But, like an average, they are not the whole story. They are just the simplest beginning of the story. With this caution in mind, we can go on to look at how some of these contrasts work.

Logic and reasoning are Yang; intuition and feeling are Yin. Therefore, in men, intellectual energy dominates; in women, emotional energy dominates. Men think with logic; women think with feeling. However, in accordance with the inevitable interchange between Yin and Yang, men think with logic but act from their emotions; women think with emotions but act from logic. There is always a balance, equilibrium, of Yin and Yang within any entity.

Heaven, Yang, is high above; earth, Yin, is low, at the bottom. Men (Yang) in general stand high, have broad vision, and tend to see a larger picture; women (Yin) are much more down-to-earth, and tend to be oriented toward practicalities of daily life. While men ponder abstract questions of the meaning, origin, and destiny of existence, women make sure that the house is clean and livable, the food is available, and the baby is fed.

Grand visions are Yang; details are Yin. Men are more ambitious, have a sense of mission, want to take on great causes and conquer the world, or want to have worldwide fame. Women, even though they have the same talents that enable men to carry out their ambitions, fundamentally focus on love, relationships, and family as the most important issues in their lives.

Yang, the energy of heaven, is dynamic and expansive; Yin, the energy of earth, is static and restrained. Men are naturally bolder, more straightforward, and persistent. Women are more sensitive, refined, and tender. Men, manifesting Yang energy, tend to be more separate in mind and body than women, who, manifesting Yin energy, tend to be more unified and integrated.

There is a long list of such general comparisons and contrasts. These all derive from the inherent difference between the Yin and Yang natures. The fact that these differences exist is a miracle and blessing. It is only when this polarity is in effect that there exists the momentum and drive that cause people to seek each other.

Unfortunately, when people do not understand or accept these differences, then differences can become a problem, even in the most everyday things. For example, men often complain that women take forever to dress before going out. A woman might try on clothes for an hour and end up wearing what she tried on first. Shopping is another situation in which these differences become visible. Men often talk about women who spend a long time trying on clothes, all of which seem great, and end up buying nothing.

Women, on the other hand, always complain that men do not want to stay home. Among working couples, apart all week, when the weekend finally comes many men want to go out, or watch sports with their buddies, rather than spend time with their wives.

These small disagreements can lead to chronic quarrels that in turn can lead to separation. Many loving couples are broken up by these small issues alone. People are very aware of this phenomenon, but the problem persists, despite all the expert advice and opinion that is easily and readily available.

The root of the problem is that, although people are aware that these differences exist, they do not understand why they exist, or genuinely accept them. They cherish the hope that their partners will, somehow, someday, change. But these differences are simply manifestations of natural law. Just as one would not want to twist nature to make trees drop leaves in the spring and grow leaves in the fall, one really should not want to change these differences between people.

Women Need Time; Men Need Space

Let's look at these differences in terms of a higher order understanding. The universe comprises time and space. Time is Yang; space is Yin. Women are inherently more connected with space (Yin), thus they naturally seek time (Yang) to complement the Yin factor. This is why women need more time. Women may spend an hour or more choosing the right clothes for an outing or social occasion; they might try on many outfits at a department store or mall. It is not an issue of "What dress should I wear?" A woman already knows what she should wear, which is why she often tries it on first. It is actually an issue of needing more time to process and assess her feelings. This is also why women are more involved with details: details are time-intensive. Men, on the other hand, need more space (Yin) to complement their inherent Yang qualities. When a man doesn't spend his free time with his wife, it doesn't mean that he doesn't love her or doesn't want to spend time with her.

Often, during courtship, men are perplexed to find that when women say "no" they sometimes mean "yes." It is true that at times, when a woman rejects a man's advances, she does not mean "no" as much as she means "not yet" or "not now." It should be emphasized that this does *not* mean that when a woman says "no" she means "yes." Rather, in courtship and in similar situations, when a woman says "no" she doesn't always mean "absolutely not." What she often does mean is that she doesn't want to be rushed, that she wants and needs time to process what is happening.

On the other hand, women often complain that during courtship men spend all their time hanging around them, but as soon as the women say "yes" and the relationship stabilizes, the men don't appear as often as they did while things were still unsettled. The men start trying to reclaim space for themselves.

This is another aspect of the same inherent difference between men and women. *Women need time, and men need space.*

Only when we understand that these are expressions of natural laws and processes can we begin to have compassion and tolerance for these differences, and to work with them.

Whether one is happy or unhappy about something is sometimes a matter of point of view: if we see the issue in terms of natural processes, we can accept it; if we see it in terms of intentional disagreeability, we find it intolerable.

I once met a beautiful dancer in Beijing who had married a popular soccer star. Unfortunately, their careers demanded that they train in different cities, and they could only be together on weekends. At first, she told me, she was very annoyed by her husband's behavior. Whenever he came home on the weekend, he would end up spending much of his time with his buddies, and not with her. After a while, she came to the conclusion that these connections were an important part of his career and his life. Instead of trying to keep him at home (which just led to quarrels and unhappiness) she started encouraging him to go out with them. Eventually, he started feeling guilty—and then he started inviting her along. It turned out that she fit really well into his circle of friends, and that when she went out with her husband and his friends, she and her husband were able to spend time with each other as well as with his larger circle of friends.

A similar but opposite case might be a husband who is always being asked by his wife to go shopping with her, and finds himself waiting with nothing to do while she tries on clothes or carefully examines all available towels or furnishings. If the husband invites a friend and his wife to accompany them, the wives can spend time shopping while the husbands spend time enjoying coffee and conversation.

These are just examples of the way that conflicts arising from the differences between men and women can be resolved. Since every couple has its own configuration, each resolution may be unique. What they all share, however, is the ability to recognize and work with the differences, rather than ignoring or suppressing them.

Yin and Yang attract and push against each other. Harmony is the state of dynamic balance of these two movements. To be in harmony does not mean that one loses its own character or identity to the other. As human beings, there is no difference between men and women. As vehicles of energy, however, men and women differ immensely. If a man becomes like his wife or girlfriend, he becomes less stimulating to her—and vice versa.

When a man has been living with a woman for a while, he often thinks he knows her. But as long as men are not women, they cannot fully understand women. *Often what we are most familiar with is what we understand least.* Familiarity is not the same as understanding.

A man will sometimes rudely cut off a woman when she tries to explain something in detail, assuming that he already knows what is going on. When a man does this, he fails in two ways. First, he thinks he knows the whole picture, but in fact may not have grasped it. Second, he misses the point that it is through detail that women process their feelings about an issue: to block the exploration of details is to disrupt this processing of feelings.

On the other side of the interaction, a woman will sometimes suspect that a man is not being forthcoming, that he is withholding his thoughts from her, and will subject him to a kind of interrogation to find out what he is thinking. But he may in fact not be thinking about anything at all. Because he does not provide a detailed account of his thoughts, the woman may feel he is withholding the details—when in fact there may not be any details. The man may be satisfied with a conclusion and a few points that establish it, and may not see any need to look further into the matter.

Let's refresh our memory of the Tai Chi diagram. Yin and Yang are relative, not absolute. Nothing is absolutely Yin or absolutely Yang. There is always Yin in Yang, and Yang in Yin. When we talk about women inherently embodying Yin energy, or men inherently embodying Yang energy, we do not mean that women are pure Yin or that men are pure Yang. It is just that women have a predominantly Yin quality, and men have a predominantly Yang quality. This might be seen as something like a seventy/thirty split.

It is a common mistake for men to think they need to be very manly to get women's attention, and for women to think they need to be very womanly to get men's attention. Of course, if a woman is not at all womanly, or a man is not at all manly, most of the time any potential connection is cut off before it can start.

Having some Yang qualities makes a woman more complete and desirable. As tenderness and refinement belong to Yin, a woman with great inner strength will complement these qualities, and will stand out because of this equilibrium. Similarly, an ideal man will have some Yin characteristics. Men stand out not merely because they are strong, but because they also have such Yin qualities as gentleness or a sense of humor. Women take male strength for granted; no one enjoys a whiny man. While women appreciate the surface strength of a man, they often fall in love with a man who has some aspect of weakness that allows them to feel they have something to offer him.

A charismatic or popular man may have thousands of admiring women around him—but he will probably surrender himself to the woman who understands his weakness.

It is a matter of balance. There should be some Yin in Yang, and some Yang in Yin.

Yin and Yang are expressed in contrasts: down/up, right/left, and mystery/familiarity. The latter is a contrast because a good relationship also requires a balance of familiarity and mystery. If two people are too familiar to each other, like brother and sister, it is hard to create a spark of romance. If they are too separate, and cannot understand each other at all, there is no basis for a romantic or loving connection.

Similarly, the question also arises about the need for absolute honesty between lovers. Mutual openness and honesty is crucial for a good relationship; however, absolute honesty is not practical. Everyone should be allowed to have his or her own secrets—and some secrets are even sacred—but otherwise it is best to be open with each other.

A contrast of Yin and Yang also exists in the contrast between jealousy and tolerance. A romantic relationship without the possibility of jealousy is incomplete. If hot and sour soup does not have vinegar in it, the flavor is incomplete.

In love and romance, there is not much difference between king and servant, or queen and handmaid: they are all manifestations of Yin and Yang energy. From the point of view of Yin and Yang, the universal energy, status, fame, wealth, and beauty (or their opposites) are not relevant. In aligning ourselves with the universal energy, we should acknowledge that we play roles, and we should acknowledge the roles we play; but we should see within them the most fundamental role, the part we play in the interaction of Yin and Yang.

When we have become aware of, and able to recognize, the interplay of Yin and Yang, we become able to work with it, rather than simply being ruled by it. We cannot step outside of it as long as we are part of existence, but we can work intelligently with it. When we have a good understanding of the interplay of Yin and Yang, we have a better basis for understanding romantic relationships.

The Wonder of Effortlessness

The usual approach to romantic relationships has a lot to do with stories we have all learned about struggling to overcome difficulties, about the need to work hard to achieve success, about triumphing over hardship. There is nothing wrong with hard work. This kind of approach works well when beginning a career, or working a farm, or mastering a craft. It does not penetrate to the inward manifestations of energy within relationships. Being guided by traditional stereotypes about relationships can make us rigid and limit our vision, making it harder to see that there is more to relationships than courtship and conquest.

A young man once complained to me about his frustration with relationships. He said that in his job, as long as he worked hard, he could be sure that his work could lead to a promotion in a fairly specific amount of time, and to a fairly orderly progress up the corporate ladder. But there was no way to be sure what he might get back from a relationship, no matter how much energy and effort he invested in it. I pointed out to him that, although this was true enough, it ignored the other side: in relationships a great deal "just happens," and does not require excessive strain or effort.

Ultimately, things follow the pattern of nature: what moves individuals is what moves the planets and the stars. This is the ultimate pattern of existence: it is not an accident, or an intrusion. It is what naturally happens. We do not need to force it, but to let it follow its own course.

We are often taught that we need to learn by studying hard; we need to learn to concentrate, to focus, and to strive. These lessons help us in some ways, but they can make for an unbalanced approach to cosmic energies. Effort and concentration are not necessarily good in themselves. Too much effort can lead us to ignore the natural course of things, or interfere unproductively with it. Too much focus can make us lose sight of the bigger picture.

Natural processes are simple and easy. In nature, things follow their own courses. Water flows downstream; fire radiates upward and outward. These things happen without effort. It is our own ignorance, and pride, that prompt us to interfere, to twist or strain the course of nature.

A successful Chinese businessman once told me that he had tried desperately to court a beautiful classmate, even following her to the United States when she went there to study, though she never paid much attention to him. After some years, when she was rejected by someone she loved, she finally agreed to marry him on the rebound. But as soon as they were married, he found himself completely disappointed. He had been attracted to her beauty, and his attraction to her was based more on vanity than on any inner connection. It is natural to work hard for what we desire, but when the desire is empty, the results of attaining it will also be empty.

Sometimes we go out of our way to get something only to find that, once we have it, it isn't what we really wanted. In fact, it is often true that something that takes unusual or extreme effort to attain is the wrong thing to aim for. This often happens in relationships.

How can we know when we are caught up in this kind of self-defeating striving? Through awareness. It is our pride and attachment that keep us from seeing the true nature and value of things, the true relationship between the energies in any situation.

Following the effortless course of nature is the key. The most important aspect of this is learning when not to try, when to let things take their own course, when and how to trust in processes outside ourselves, and outside our direct control. We need to learn, as the old saying goes, how to make haste slowly—to accept a point of view in which we are small, and carried by the great currents of life.

But if effortless simplicity is really all there is to it, why doesn't everyone allow themselves to be carried by the currents of life? Why is there so much fruitless struggling? And why do people continue to struggle?

The Source Within

The reason we keep struggling is that we have forgotten something very important about our world. We are like people who look into a mirror thinking we are looking through a window. We have come to think that the reflected scene is the only scene there is, and that it is the real scene.

The mirror world we have taken for the real world is what we call the "outer" world, the world that we experience through our six senses.

However, in reality, all understanding and all manifestation move from inward to outward. Everything begins with awareness: we have six senses so that we can see, hear, smell, taste, feel, and think. This provides the basis for us to recognize and relate to the universe, to recognize our own existence.

But because our six senses allow us to receive information from outside, we come to feel that what we know comes from the outside. We assume that we learn more from focusing our attention outward than from paying attention to what's going on within. We think that the objects of awareness are the source of awareness. This is the beginning of many difficulties.

For one thing, the information from outside is subject to all sorts of distortion. We do not have direct access to what is going on outside us, but our perceptions create impressions, and we use our impressions to form judgments about what is going on. We then forget that we have done this, and identify our impressions with what is outside, no matter how accurate or inaccurate these impressions may be. We are often like people who see a rope and mistake it for a snake, and because of our shock and fear decide that it must be a snake, without ever pausing to reflect on how we formed the impression or the judgment.

Although awareness should begin within, with awareness of ourselves, there are reasons why we tend to look in the wrong place. First, we do not look inside because our senses focus—or seem to focus—outward. Furthermore, we have developed certain self-protective mechanisms, layers of screening that protect us from what could become (or what we are afraid could become) paralyzing self-doubt.

Unfortunately, this tendency to protect ourselves leads to an unconscious bias or distortion in our sense of ourselves. But accurate self-awareness is crucial: it provides a fundamental basis for our actions in the world. We need to know our inherent strengths and weaknesses—physical, emotional, and intellectual. Knowing this, we can choose the right direction. Knowing that you are only of average height gives you some useful information about whether to try to become a professional basketball player. Knowing that you are an introvert (and don't feel like changing) gives you useful information about whether a job in sales would be suitable.

Looking outward is Yang; looking inward is Yin. Our usual habits are heavily biased in favor of Yang; only by correcting this imbalance can we gain a more accurate picture of who, and what, we really are.

The First Relationship

In discussing loving relationships between people, we should begin with the fundamental relationship, the relationship one has with oneself. To do this, we must cultivate self-awareness.

We are happy when we feel that other people know and accept us—but we cannot know whether or not they really do unless we know ourselves.

Developing self-awareness begins with basic things, such as becoming aware of breathing. Breathing is one of the most powerful aspects of human existence. Breath is the gate between life and death. From awareness of breathing we become aware of our emotions, thoughts, values, strengths, weaknesses, talents, and handicaps, as well as our physical capacities.

It is also important to be aware, from moment to moment, of our thoughts. This is one of the most powerful tools for improving and transcending ourselves. When we are angry, the moment we become aware of our anger, the anger can be dissolved. People generally find it hard to look in the mirror and yell at themselves.

Getting to know oneself is the beginning of establishing a relationship with oneself. This awareness should not just be static: it should be an awareness of our dynamic patterns, of how we change, of what has led us to where we are, and what influences us at the moment to continue to change into new or different patterns. As we cultivate this kind of awareness, we also become more conscious of the rigidities and resistances that block us from adapting smoothly to what is going on around us. This awareness can help us dissolve these obstructions and become more flexible, more adaptable. We become more aware of the same patterns in other people, and we come to understand their behavior as though it were our own.

When we begin to cultivate self-awareness, we form opinions and judgments. There are things we can accept or even enjoy, and things we refuse to accept. But with deeper awareness, the constant presence of things we don't enjoy leads us to recognize that we cannot simultaneously be aware of and resist, or flinch away from, awareness. It is human nature to seek pleasant things and avoid unpleasant things. But what is "unpleasantness"? What makes something "negative"? Whether something is ugly or beautiful, or comfortable or uncomfortable, depends not only on the thing but on our perception of it. A snake and an eel are very similar, but fishermen love eels and hate snakes. Many people find caterpillars creepy, but people who raise silkworms (which, after all, are caterpillars) find them very beautiful. Once the reaction and the perception are both held in awareness, it becomes clearer that there is no necessary connection between a particular thing and a particular reaction to it. These connections come from the person who experiences the event, and as the person's values and perceptions change, the experience can also change.

It is important to be able to accept and recognize what is happening in any moment of experience. Only by doing so is it possible to have an accurate understanding of that moment.

Many of our likes and dislikes derive from certain kinds of attachments. It is inevitable that in any imaginable real world there will be differences, and these differences can be seen as distance from some standard, either "better" or "worse."

In nature, there are tall trees, shrubs, and grass. Each one has its own place and its own way of growing. Some people might feel that grass is "common" because it spreads horizontally, not nobly upward like a giant tree. But does grass—or the tall tree—feel this way? Grass undoubtedly feels at home being grass, and trees feel quite ordinary being trees.

The same thing is true with inward characteristics. If, when you look inward, you find something disgusting or appalling, do not flinch away, or try to see something else instead. That revolting sight is what is there at the moment:

it should be held in awareness, not pushed out of it. This does not mean, however, that you should hold onto it and refuse to let it go.

Divine Acceptance

In the *Tao Teh Ching*, it is said that we should learn from the earth. What does earth teach us? Earth teaches acceptance. Everything we discard, we give to the earth, and the earth accepts it and transmutes it. In turn, the earth provides us support and grows things to nourish us. Without acceptance, there can be no giving, no transformation, no love.

We find it hard to accept things that are negative, imperfect, ugly, and so on. No one, of course, is fully satisfied with himself or herself. Life is full of imperfections, and the inevitability of those imperfections is hard to accept. But imperfection is the impetus, the motivation, for all action, for all creation. If the world were perfect, there would be nothing to do, nothing to achieve. Dedication to art, music, literature, poetry, or scientific discovery comes from the struggle with imperfection. The fruits of all this work help us see the value and beauty of imperfection.

Before we can ask people to accept us or love us, we have to be able to accept, and love, ourselves, and be grateful for what we are. Our imperfections are not things to be complacent about, but things that lead us to move toward something better. When we can realize this with regard to ourselves, we can realize it with regard to others—and they, in turn, can realize it with regard to us.

Being able to accept and love oneself is just the beginning of the story. Accepting the reality of the moment does not mean sticking to that moment. Only if the train comes into the station can it move on to the next station. We accept what is so that our actions can be grounded in what is there. To accept the reality of the present situation does not mean being limited by it; it means knowing the place from which one starts, and when that is known, the next thing to do is to begin the journey.

Sometimes a mistake has been made, and reality has changed as a result, but we find it hard to accept, and lose energy brooding about what could or should have happened. This is simply a waste of time and energy. Things that exist cannot be wished away: they have to be worked with, to change the situation to what it could and should become.

Change is the only unchanging feature of existence. We should constantly accept, and constantly move beyond. We develop to the extent that we can accept; to the extent that we accept where and what we are, we develop beyond that point.

To be aware, to accept, and to achieve—this is the fundamental preparation for us to establish good, loving relationships with people. It is the beginning—and the end as well.

Successful relationships are not about obtaining something outside ourselves. They are about manifesting what is within ourselves in ways that fit with what is being manifested by others around us. In nature, things happen easily and simply. If we find ourselves grasping and struggling, we are probably trying to force things against nature. When we are well prepared, things that are in harmony with us naturally come to us.

This is why we should first focus on making ourselves harmonious and affectionate, able to have a good relationship with ourselves. To the extent that we prepare ourselves, we become like a radio station, broadcasting our joy and happiness to the world, to all radios that are tuned to the same frequency. By starting with this, we start with what we have the most control over: our own character, actions, and reactions. When we have deepened our understanding of our own feelings and reactions, we can begin to work with the outside factors that affect us, because we will be able to perceive these effects more accurately.

3

Your Place or Mine?

The right time, the right place, and the right people: these are the essential ingredients for success in any human endeavor. If any one ingredient is inadequate, it will be a long uphill journey to reach the goal. If any two ingredients are missing, any attempt to reach the goal is simply wishful thinking.

Place is one of the essential factors for any human endeavor—and thus, naturally, for love and romantic relationships. This is why it is crucial to discuss place, which is linked with the principle of earth, the element associated with nourishment, connection, support, and protection.

While we focused on human factors in the previous chapter (emotions, intelligence, and so on), it is important to understand that we are part of nature, and that every human characteristic is intimately linked with features of the greater whole, the universe. The human body is an open system. The universe is also an open system. We are always in the greater whole, and permeable to it; it is always permeable to us. *We cannot exist beyond or outside of place.*

We Are What We Live In

The genetic traits that make up the differences between human beings are the result of evolutionary processes that were shaped by various specific natural environments. Genetic traits can take millions of years to form. But environments also have impacts on nongenetic traits, and these have been observed and recorded for thousands of years, in many volumes of Feng Shui classics. The spatial environment shapes our character, personality, and emotions.

Everyone is aware that we respond to our environment. A small, enclosed place or an open, expansive place evoke different emotions and responses. A high place with a great view or a low valley with limited visibility also affect us differently. In a restaurant, sitting next to the entrance or kitchen door feels very different from sitting in a secure, quiet corner. This is why, in any private or public space, we intuitively choose some spots over others.

Places also affect people on the group level. Groups of people will exhibit clear differences depending on whether they live in a big city, near a great body of water, on high desert, or in rough mountains. City dwellers think, act, and associate differently than people who live in the country, even if they share the same culture and religion. City people tend to be more witty, shrewd, and self-indulgent; mountain people tend to be observant, relaxed, and reserved. There are even differences between people who live in different kinds of mountains: people who live in barren mountains tend to be more direct, rude, or even violent than people who live in lush, forested mountains.

Energy Manifests Reality

How does this come about? What is the fundamental influence behind these differences? Scholars in many fields throughout history have come up with explanations in terms of religion, culture, geography, or climatic patterns. To see the fundamental causal factors, we need to look at things in terms of higher order principles.

According to Feng Shui concepts, these differences are due to the fundamental factor or universal essence called "qi" (also spelled "chi") in Chinese. According to Chinese metaphysics, the essential, finest element of the universe is qi. It is said that qi has no form and no image: it is smaller than anything that can be imagined, and at the same time permeates everything on a scale far beyond any ability to imagine. Everything that manifests is a transformation and manifestation of qi. Qi becomes form, and form becomes qi.

Qi cannot be measured, seen, cut up, or put in a box. It is not a "thing" like a piece of wood or stone, or a cup of water. Qi is a name for something that is recognized in many traditions, though each tradition gives it a different name—prana, qi, pneuma, etheric energy, spirit, and so on. In the Bible, the story of the creation of Adam involves God blowing the breath of life into Adam.

People sometimes call this "life energy." But according to traditional Chinese concepts, life energy is only one aspect or manifestation of qi. Qi is understood to be the organizing energy behind every kind of manifestation, living and nonliving, sentient and nonsentient, large or small.

Form Defines Energy

For examples, let's look at the simple images of the square and circle (figure 3.1).

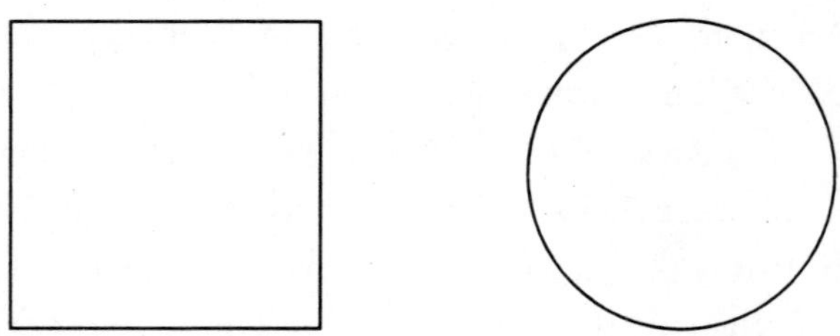

Figure 3.1: Square and circle

Most of us looking at these two images realize that we get distinctly different feelings from them. This must mean that the images have an impact, psychological or physiological, on us. Why is this? We might say that these two images project different kinds of qi, or energy, to us, and cause different responses.

If these two-dimensional diagrams can make such a difference, then the three-dimensional world we live in, with all its various forms, must be constantly influencing us even more.

When people are happy, their lips tend to turn upward; when they are sad, their lips tend to turn downward. The shape or position of the lips manifests different energies according to the form they take in facial expressions. In the same way, a beautiful face or a plain face, a child jumping around or an old person walking bent over all manifest different *forms,* and reveal different kinds of energy. We can see these forms in people, and in rooms, houses, and places. We can also see the different compositions of landscapes in the same way. Mountains, small hills, flat ground, and rivers and lakes—all these manifest different energies according to their forms, and have characteristic effects on the people who live with them.

In this chapter, we focus in the impact of our immediate living spaces—our house or the room we live in, for example. The form of a house—its relative size, shape, floor plan, design (as well as its color, furnishings, and decoration)—naturally has a very direct effect on the people who live there. It affects our health, emotional state, prosperity, and, of course, our relationships, including our romantic relationships.

The age-old question "Your place or my place?" may have deeper implications than most people realize.

An Ideal House for Love and Romance

What kind of house or dwelling can nurture loving relationships?

In Feng Shui terms, a place affects relationships, health, and prosperity. It naturally affects romantic relationships as well, but it is not possible to separate any of these specific effects from the overall effect. Feng Shui is a holographic approach, and looks at the whole system, not just a fragment of it.

An ideal house is a house with an abundance of qi. This will manifest in a *good location*, a *wholesome form*, a *smooth energy flow,* and a *warm or affectionate quality.*

Good location means a balanced and harmonious environment. In the classical terminology of Feng Shui, this means that four features are involved: the *Dragon, Guardian, Energy Spot,* and *Water.* The Dragon refers to support behind the house. This support can consist of a small hill, a building, or even a flat area—rather than, say, a cliff or ravine. The Guardian refers to companion structures on either side of the house, which should not be isolated or hemmed in by overbearing buildings or crowded, cramped structures. The Energy Spot is where the house or building sits: it should be well protected and wholesomely configured, so that energy can collect and coagulate. The Water refers to the open space that should be in front of the building, allowing energy to come in and collect, and allowing for projection, expansion, and breadth of vision on the part of those who live there.

Wholesome form means that the building should be strongly integrated and pleasant-looking, and not too strange or disturbing, regardless of its size or the materials used. It should not be too choppy or fragmented, even from a bird's-eye view or a side view. The floor plan of a residence should be generally rectangular or square.

A smooth energy flow is related to the partitions and layout of the building. The interior space should not be too open, as in one big room, or too confined, broken up, or confusing, like a maze. Each room of the house should be well connected to the energy flowing through the house.

A warm and affectionate quality refers to the feeling of abundance and comfort that some places seem to give people for no apparent reason. Our energy bodies intuitively respond to the energy of a space. If the energy of a space resonates well with our own energy, we will feel comfortable even if we cannot pin down a reason for the feeling. In general, if the former three conditions (location, form, and energy flow) are fulfilled, you will probably feel a definite warm quality in the place.

Wholesome form brings forth wholesome energy, and has a wholesome effect. These energetic qualities are all manifestations of the form or structure of the immediate environment, and of the layout, size, and shape of the building. This is the basic requirement for an ideal house, and thus for good relationships, prosperity, and health.

With these criteria fulfilled, we can then look at more specific elements.

The Main Entrance: The Key to Differentiating Masculine and Feminine

The *main entrance* is the face of the house, defining the energy character of the house. It defines the Yin-Yang configuration of the house, and determines whether the house is more masculine or feminine. In addition, the main entrance is like the human face: it naturally reveals the social character and personality. A door that directly faces the street gives a more direct, straightforward quality than one that is turned ninety degrees, which gives a more obscure or retiring feeling. A door should be clear, strong, stable, and easily visible, not hidden away.

When the main entrance is in the center, as in most traditional houses, left and right are equal—that is, Yang and Yin are balanced, and their qualities manifest in a balanced way. If the main energy shifts too far toward one side or the other, an imbalance is created. If the door is on the left side of the house (as you stand inside and look out), the mass of the house expresses itself more as Yin energy, and will be more nourishing to other Yin qualities. This is a "feminine house," and it is more likely that the people who live in such a house will manifest more feminine force.

On the other hand, if the door is closer to the right corner (again, from the inside looking out), this is a "masculine house," one that is dominated by masculine forces and will be more supportive to Yang energies; it will not provide as much support to feminine energies.

What does door location have to do with Yin and Yang energies? It is directly related to the flow of energy within the house, either clockwise or counterclockwise. When energy flows clockwise, the force is Yang; when counterclockwise, it is Yin, as shown in figure 3.2.

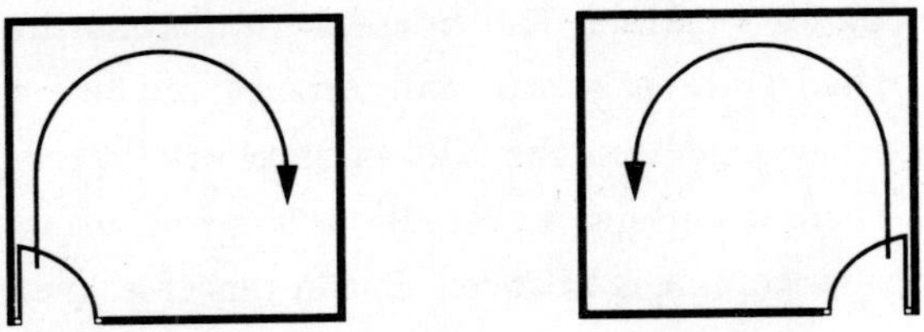

Figure 3.2: Masculine house (left) and feminine house (right)

A woman who yearns for a relationship, and who finds that she is living in a very feminine house, might well consider looking for a different place to live, one with a door more or less in the center.

This is of course a somewhat simplified picture: we have focused on the house, but the house itself can be influenced by larger environmental influences, such as neighborhood, climate, and the larger geography, as well as by factors that are specific to Feng Shui. The issue can quickly become too complex to deal with in this book.

Once, I was consulting with a very successful physician who lived in Caracas, Venezuela, with her two children.

She initially told me that she asked for a consultation just to get a general overview of their house. I went through the whole house and made suggestions. As I was ready to conclude and say goodbye, she nervously asked me about how the house could affect relationships. This was actually one of the pressing reasons she had asked for the consultation. Divorced for three years, she was desperately yearning for a partner. This house, with the door in the center, had a nice, balanced main entrance, but for convenience they were using the side entrance, next to the carport. There is nothing necessarily wrong with using the side entrance, if it is balanced. But in this case, the side entrance was unbalanced, and using it shifted the energy balance of the house radically toward the feminine side, which did not help nourish masculine energies. Since it was not difficult for them to use the original main entrance as their customary entrance, I suggested that they do so to bring about a more balanced manifestation of Yin and Yang energies. I saw her again six months later in one of my workshops, accompanied by her new boyfriend.

One of my clients told me that her house was really ideal in Feng Shui terms: it had a good mountain (Dragon) and Guardians, and the door was in the center, balancing Yin and Yang. Yet she was still having trouble finding a partner. In examining the floor plan of her house, I found that not only was her bedroom door behind her bed, but so was the main house entrance door. In other words, her bed was in a position that faced her away from the main entrance. This compounded the problem of a lack of connection with the outside. The energy was balanced, but there was no connection with the outside, so the energy did not flow.

For this reason, although the position of the door is usually a very reliable indicator, the concept should not be accepted rigidly, or on faith, since there are many other factors that can influence how this pattern manifests. It is important to test this concept for oneself, to find how and when it is true in a straightforward fashion, and how and when it is modified by other circumstances.

In the old days, most houses had their main entrance in the center. Most family relationships were stable; they would end only with the death of one member of the couple. It was rare for a man or a woman to live alone. The increase in unbalanced houses, with main doors far to the left or right, has come with an increase in unbalanced and unstable relationships, and an abundance of single men and women. Many of the struggles people have in their relationships can be correlated to this sort of imbalance. This is not to say that the position of the door causes or compels people to have unbalanced relationships, but rather that there is a connection between the two, no matter which one comes first in time.

The Bedroom: Nest of Nourishment

The *bedroom* affects relationships, health, and emotions. Since we spend a third of our lives in bed, it is bound to have a marked impact. The size and the form of the bedroom have a great deal to do with this impact. The most relevant feature is the qi of the room, which is directly associated with the space. A room that is too large can create a dispersal of energy; a room that is too small might not provide a good flow of energy. Size affects the quantity of qi flow; form affects the quality. The bedroom should be square or rectangular, and not consist of sharply broken-up spaces. Form defines energy: wholesome forms provide wholesome energy, and unwholesome or chaotic forms provide chaotic energy.

Of the features of the bedroom, the most important is the placement of the bed. The fundamental rule is that the head of the bed should be directly against a solid wall, as shown in figure 3.3.

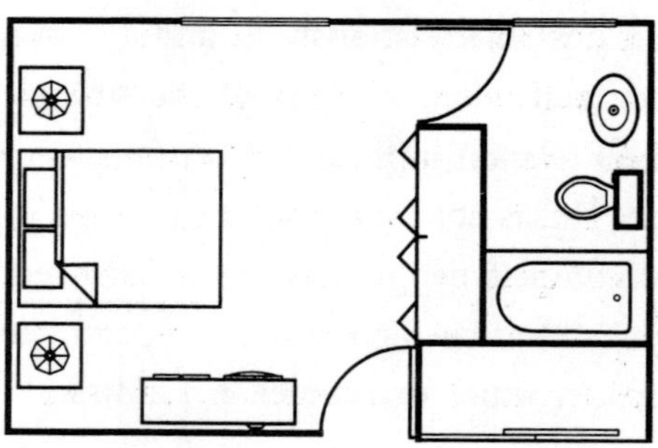

Figure 3.3: Ideal bedroom layout

There should not be a door directly in front of or directly behind the bed. Nor should there be one next to the head of the bed on either side. There are many other ideas about how a bed should be oriented. Some people say that it should align with the magnetic north; others, that it should be aligned east and west, with the course of the sun; and still others, that the bed should be oriented in accordance with the birthday of the person who sleeps in it. These ideas might have validity in particular circumstances, in particular cultural contexts. But from a real Feng Shui point of view, positioning the bed in terms of the form and layout of the space is much more important. The effect from designing according to the form and layout of the space is greater than the effect from considering orientation and placement alone.

One of the most common sources of a negative effect on a relationship is a big window directly behind the bed; it's as if the energy moving to the bed spills out the window rather than circulating and nourishing the people who sleep in the bed. Energy can drain away from the relationship. Even if the couple do not fight or argue, they may just live together in a conventional relationship with no real connection between them. Simply blocking or covering such a window can easily improve this situation.

It is important to have some windows in the bedroom, but since the bedroom should be more Yin (in contrast to the living room or kitchen, which are naturally more Yang), it should not have too many windows, since this would make it too Yang. If there are too many windows, it is important to seal some of them off. Window blinds or even drapes will help, but may not do the job completely. It may be necessary to hang paintings over some windows to cover them up, or use another method to block or conceal them.

These simple rules about form and layout are the most important; other considerations are minor at best. If you follow these rules, you will have dealt with the most important aspects of bedroom configuration.

The Kitchen: Harmonizing Water and Fire

The *kitchen* is closely related to male/female relationships, and to the management of household finances. The most important features of the kitchen are the sink/faucet (water) and the stove (fire). These two are linked with Yin and Yang, and thus with female and male energies. How these two features are placed, and how they relate to each other, have direct consequences for the relationships between the males and females living in the house, and have an effect on the control of money as well. The most ideal placement of these two features is at a ninety-degree angle, with the stove against a solid wall and the sink against a wall with a window above it. It is also acceptable to have the stove and the sink side-by-side, as shown in figure 3.4

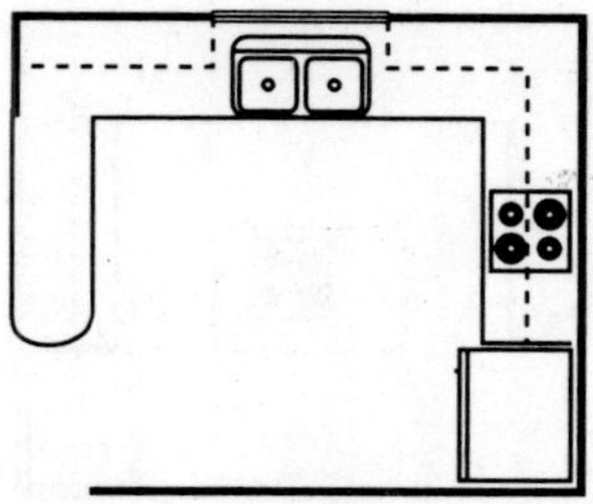

Figure 3.4: Ideal stove/faucet layout

This has been the traditional layout, for good (though often unconscious) reasons. Our ancestors may have been more in tune with their intuitions than the people who design our modern kitchens.

Over the past thirty years in the United States, a new form has been created for the sake of novelty: the "island kitchen." As houses get bigger, and kitchens also get bigger, the island is convenient as a workplace and an extended seating or storage place. This is fine. However, when the stove is placed in the island, this creates serious problems. With this arrangement, the sink and stove almost always confront each other, and this affects the relationships between males and females in such a house: it will be, to say the least, more challenging. It should be possible for an enterprising statistician to establish the correlation between rate of divorce and incidence of island kitchens with stoves in the island, as in figure 3.5.

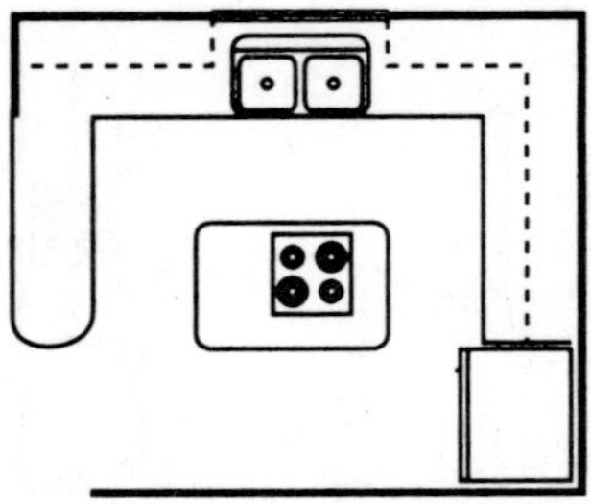

Figure 3.5: Not an ideal stove/faucet layout

Usually, if a design does not make sense in terms of Feng Shui, it does not make practical sense either. An island kitchen with the stove in the island is not reasonable from an ergonomic point of view. You have to wonder if the people who came up with this idea ever did very much cooking.

I once visited a house in a very secure, protected neighborhood inside a country club that included a golf course. The house was well built, and the furniture was chosen and arranged with great, almost impeccable, taste. The smiling, middle-aged couple that lived there received me and led me through the house. As we entered the kitchen, they told me that they had moved in three years ago. As soon as I noticed the opposing arrangement of the stove and sink in the kitchen, I asked them if they had relationship and money issues. Their smiles disappeared, and they began to tell me the problems they had begun to have after moving into the house. They had asked for this consultation because they were ready to sell the house, and they were hoping that my suggestions and advice could help them sell it. The problem that I saw concerned their island kitchen, in which the stove and the sink directly confronted each other, and in which there was no support behind the stove. Even more, with a ravine behind the house, there was no support for the house. This compounded the negative impact of the lack of support for the stove. A basic understanding of Feng Shui principles would suggest that money was inevitably going to be an issue in the relationship—and that would lead to other conflicts.

It is often the case that things manifest in fairly simple patterns. However, there are no rigid rules, and it is not my intention to present any rigid do's or don'ts and their necessary consequences. In assessing a house, one must always look at the whole picture. If there is one mistake, but all other features are solid, the one mistake might not be enough to manifest any negative consequences. At the same time, an accumulation of small mistakes, individually not too serious, could have grave consequences. And an accumulation of big mistakes will definitely have negative consequences.

For example: if the sink (water) and stove (fire) directly face each other, and the couple have a big window directly behind their bed, and the main door is too far to the left or the right corner of the house, then there is a good chance that the relationship of that couple will either end in divorce or dissolve into a paper relationship. Try looking around at the couples you know and check to see if this idea has any substance.

Furnishing and Decorating: Reflections of the Inner World

Furnishing and decorating a house is like applying color to the structure of a painting. Both affect the sense of liveliness, and often reflect the values, status, personalities, and emotional states of the residents. Furnishings and decorations in a house are direct manifestations of the inner world of those who live there.

People with abundant life energy manifest this in the furnishings and decorations they choose; people who are depressed and lonely do the same.

While consulting at the home of a very shy computer programmer, I noticed that every wall in every room had only a single thing hanging on it, and each picture had only a single subject. I told her, "I don't see any images of pairs," leaving unspoken the second part of the thought, "so how can I expect to see any pairing for you?"

These outward manifestations come from inner realities. This doesn't mean that hanging a picture of a pair of birds will necessarily bring a partner. But it does mean that even hanging a picture of a pair of birds signals a change in inward energy, which might manifest later in outward ways.

In doing a consultation for a very charming young flight attendant, I found that, on entering the door of her apartment, the kitchen was on the right; on the left wall, there hung an African mask: a male head and a female head pushed together, with the top part of the heads missing. In the living room, there was a painting of a woman with a sad, lonely face. Next to that was a print of a mountain, with the bottom part of the mountain broken off. Without asking any personal questions, I could tell that she had been trying hard, and unsuccessfully, to make a relationship work. The broken-off mountain suggested that the relationship did not have a solid base of support. The sad face resonated with her struggles in forming relationships. These images told a whole story about her—one that turned out to be true.

I suggested that she remove these three art objects and replace them with nature scenes or images of plants, flowers, or animals. I suggested that she change an overhanging black cabinet in the kitchen, which was creating a sense of pressure, and also recommended certain adjustments in her bedroom.

Just by hearing me point out my observations and make suggestions, she commented, she could already sense that change was taking place. But how could such small changes in decor change her love life? Remember: a picture is a manifestation of inner energy and inner reality. As we explained in the Tai Chi diagram, cause and effect are not absolutely distinguished, and effects can become causes. The outer reality is a manifestation of what is within—but changing what is outside can also change what is within.

The Plum-Flower Corner: Extra Feng Shui Mileage?

In China, people believe that houseplants and flowers can enhance romance, so they often suggest placing fresh flowers or houseplants in a particular place in the house, called the "Plum-Flower Corner." This is supposed to enhance romantic relationships, because the plants in that place act like a matchmaker.

There are many different approaches to determining where this Plum-Flower Corner is. For example, according to one approach, in houses that face south, the Plum-Flower Corner is on the east side of the house. In houses that face west, it is on the south; in houses that face north, it is on the west; in houses that face east, it is on the north. Another approach is based on birth year and Chinese zodiacal sign. For people born in the years of the Rat, Dragon, or Monkey, the Plum-Flower Corner is in the west. For people born in the years of the Ox, Snake, or Rooster, it is in the south. For people born in the years of the Tiger, Horse, or Dog, it is in the east. For those born in the years of the Rabbit, Sheep, or Pig, it is in the north. (The relationship between sign and birth year is explained in chapter 4.) The fundamental idea is that you should place a fresh-cut flower or houseplant in the appropriate place to enhance the romantic relationship of the people who live in the house.

Some people even overstretch this idea and worry about the right colors for the flowers, the right shape for the vase, and so on. Many of these considerations are irrelevant: the important thing is the plant or flower itself, which is what brings forth the good energy, the beneficial "information."

There are similar concepts in other cultures, but these are all culturally rooted practices. True Feng Shui concepts are universal, not tied to any specific cultural package. Nonetheless, culturally specific practices also have their own validity, since they connect with factors that are important in the lives of people who live within those cultures.

One of the qualities of flowers and plants is their fragrance, and fragrance has a direct impact on emotions. People often use fragrance to enhance or stimulate romantic feelings, but it is important not to overdo it.

When your house has abundant energy and an affectionate, comfortable quality, you will naturally resonate with it. Resonating with those energies, you will draw to yourself the kind of relationships manifested by those energies.

Leave Room to Breathe

In furnishing a house, there are many points people can focus on. One of the important ones is to keep a balance between the amount of occupied and unoccupied space (in line with the balance between Yang and Yin). Furnishings should not be too sparse; nor should they be excessive. A bare house does not allow for any expression, but a house that is overstuffed is an indication that something is missing in the lives of the people in the house. In one case, it may be that there is little to express; in the other, there is an attempt to fill a void or to cover it up and avoid recognizing it.

Decorations and ornamentation often reflect the inner state of the people who live in a place. When I visited the house of a very successful chef in Puerto Rico, I saw that her home was filled with wonderful art and decorations that she had collected around the world. In fact, there were fine pieces of art in every available space. She wondered why, despite her success, her life still lacked any romantic connection. I asked her if she could point out any unoccupied or empty space available in her house. Completely filling up one's environment often reflects a heart that is too occupied to allow any outside connection. At the same time, when people feel emptiness in their lives, they often compensate by filling up their environment. Is one the cause and the other the effect?

When something is missing in the heart, a success-oriented woman may try to compensate by filling the spaces in her life with other things or activities: but the more her life is filled up, the less chance there is for the missing element to find a way in. Sometimes it is necessary to accept solitude in order to have enough space to allow others to enter one's life. People are often afraid that accepting solitude means being lonely—but solitude is not loneliness.

Mirrors Don't Have Artificial Intelligence Yet

Some popular Feng Shui manuals in the United States put heavy emphasis on mirrors, hailing them as "the aspirin of Feng Shui." They are said to cure almost every possible problem. But thinking that mirrors can absorb good energy and repel bad energy involves making the odd assumption that they have some sort of intelligence or programming that can tell the difference between good and bad. This is especially odd because our modern mirrors have only existed for a few centuries.

In reality, mirrors do have practical uses: they can create an illusion of larger space, reflect more light into a place, and—most important—they give us a chance to adjust our clothes and makeup.

Much of the Feng Shui popularly taught in the United States emphasizes the application of mirrors. However, not only do mirrors *not* have the magical power to create positive forces, they can actually make things worse. We should be very thoughtful about how we use mirrors. We should use them only when they are clearly necessary. Mirrors create false images and impressions, disorient the mind, and create confusion. If you like to get into arguments, try sitting next to a mirror wall with a good friend. Remember: when you look into a mirror, you only see your own image.

In recent years, builders in the United States have installed mirrored closet doors. Every new house seems to have one in the bedroom. This feature often creates stress and disorientation. If you have one and think it does not bother you, try covering it for a while. You will probably feel much calmer and more relaxed with it covered.

The pervasive use of mirrors and the emphasis on them as a Feng Shui cure or device is a new fashion in the United States. But mirrors did not play an important role in traditional Feng Shui practice, and they do not play an important role in modern Feng Shui practice. This claim that mirrors are beneficial has no historical background, and it doesn't make much sense, either.

Often people accept such ideas on pure faith, even though they may feel that the ideas do not make sense. But it's important to remember that Feng Shui involves universal principles according to what everyone already understands—what we call "common sense." When a Feng Shui "expert" tells you something, check with your own inner feelings. When you can really tune into your own intuition, you can be your own Feng Shui master.

I once visited the home of a designer, a very beautiful and talented woman who was helping me with a book. All the features of her house were ideal: a balanced main entrance, a balanced and protected bedroom, and an ideal kitchen layout. Since the house had a great balance of energy, I wondered why there was no man in the house. When I asked her, she told me that she had been married when she and her husband had moved into the house three years ago. Shortly afterward, they began arguing a lot. Her husband moved out, and they divorced. During our conversation, I noticed that the whole wall of the kitchen nook was covered with a grid mirror. No wonder they argued! I suggested that she remove the grid mirror, and paint the wall a solid color. Mirrors often bring confusion due to the doubling of images; grid mirrors can create even more turbulence, and this can affect the emotional states of people who are around them for a prolonged period. Within a few months after she removed the mirror and painted the wall, she was madly in love again.

Pink Is Not the Color for Romance

People live in sunshine, and thus live among colors. Because we live among colors, in every moment we respond to them. If we find that we do not like the color of some piece of clothing, no matter how good the style or how beautiful the fabric, we will probably not buy it.

Many studies have looked at the impact of colors on human emotions. Color affects the perception of volume, weight, and size. Light colors make you feel a room is larger; dark colors make it seem smaller. Black objects feel heavier; light or less saturated objects feel lighter. Colors also affect the perception of temperature: this is why people divide colors into warm (such as red and orange) and cool (such a blue and green). But most important are the physiological and psychological effects of color.

Red is exciting, passionate, aggressive, and intense; it also stimulates the nervous system and increases adrenaline production. Orange is stimulating, lively, and intrusive. Yellow is cheerful, high-spirited, and glaring; it stimulates the digestive system. Green is relaxing, reflective, and common or tiresome. Blue is relaxing, calming, or depressing and cold; it helps create balanced physical states. Purple is dignified, or conceited and lonely.

Having said this, the impact of color on people in houses, or in rooms in a house, is a much more complicated issue than can be predicted by simple associations. The effect of color is influenced by culture and heritage, and also by economic, geographic, and religious factors, as well as by taste and educational level. Color cannot be isolated from substance: the red of a rose has a different effect on people than does the red of blood.

The key point about color in the house is the total volume of exposure. If you wear red clothes, you actually see red directly only when you put your clothes on and take them off; otherwise the red color is very much in the background of your consciousness. On the other hand, if you paint a room red, you are confronted with the color wherever you turn, as long as you are in the room. It is the same color, but the effects will be very different because the amount of exposure is different. Overexposure to a color can easily create color-fatigue, and a kind of undernourishment from other colors. Remember: when you see only one color you are actually missing the other six major colors of the spectrum.

Much research has been done in modern times about the psychological and physiological impact of colors on people. This research often fails to address the matter of the volume of exposure. This is one reason that real life applications are not as simple as laboratory results would suggest. Traditional Feng Shui approaches things from a more general level, from the perspective of Yin and Yang. It might see colors in terms of heavy or light, cold or warm, constraining or expanding, and so on. This is why a floor should, in general, be darker than a ceiling: what is light (Yang) should be on the top, and what is heavy (Yin) should be on the bottom.

Associations of particular colors with specific qualities or applications quickly become mechanical and rigid, and can have negative effects. Many popular Feng Shui manuals associate certain qualities with certain colors: knowledge with blue, fame with red, luck with gray, and so on. People claim that such connections can be traced back to the ancient Chinese Ba Gua concept. But in fact, anyone with a basic knowledge of Ba Gua Theory and with the *I Ching* (the *Book of Changes,* one of the most ancient and important books in Chinese history) knows that there is no theoretical or historical basis for these claims, nor do they reflect any kind of traditional practice. Furthermore, the rigid application of specific correlations does not make practical or common sense. It can only create confusion, if not problems, especially if applied in a house.

It is generally best to use very simple color schemes. If people aren't sure what color to use, they should stay with off-white or beige. This may seem a bit dull to people who have read many books about complicated color correspondences, and who want to use everything they have read. One of my students told me that she thought I was oversimplifying things, so when she painted her house, she painted her bedroom pink. But as soon as it was done, she began to feel so uncomfortable that she had to repaint it. Pink colors might incite romantic feelings when on a greeting card or a rose, but a bedroom painted pure pink will be too overwhelming, creating a sense of overintense excitement that will generate anxiety rather than romance. This is something my readers can validate for themselves!

Appropriate color has to do with the size of the room, the amount of light in the room, and the function of the room. Lighter colors are more appropriate when the room needs a Yang influence; darker or cooler colors when it needs a Yin influence. But there is no easy way to say that any particular color is always better or worse for a particular room without making very misleading generalizations. If you enjoy a particular color, use it—just don't cover the whole room with it. Instead, paint it on the side you would normally look at least.

Yin and Yang Revisited: Looking Inward and Looking Outward

We have been trying to address the issue of good Feng Shui in a house without getting overwhelmed by details. Whether a house has good Feng Shui has nothing to do with how expensive, how grand, or how large it is. The key, as we have said, is having good energy: a good location, a wholesome form, and a smooth energy flow will produce a sense of abundance and affection.

Let's get back to the basics. A house should be clean and orderly. Since form defines energy, a clean and orderly space brings forth clean and orderly energy. If a place is messy, cluttered, dirty, or chaotic, it will naturally bring forth chaotic energy. If your partner is always avoiding coming home, look to see if this is an issue.

What makes a place warm and affectionate? Most people think of this in terms of visual factors: good furniture, interesting colors, or nice decorations. The actual key is the qi of the house, which is defined by the form and layout of the house. A very fancy, well-decorated house filled with amenities might still make you feel cold; a simple house with a good layout and design can give a feeling of warmth.

When a house is too partitioned and broken up, and lacks well-placed windows, the flow tends to stagnate. Without proper flow, energy becomes scarce. On the other hand, if the space is not well defined, or is too open (if there are big windows too closely facing the entrance, for example), energy flows out too quickly and does not stay in the house. Without an abundance of qi, there is no sense of warmth.

A clean and orderly house, with appropriately defined and smoothly connected interior spaces, will have good energy flow that can be enhanced by appropriate furniture arrangement. Thoughtful use of color can make the space even more inviting. Without this basic quality, though, changes in furnishings and decoration will not help much.

The key to good furnishings is balance and simplicity. The usual mistake is to overcrowd the furniture, overdo the decorations, and make the color scheme too busy. *Simple is better; less is more.* In a room, if one wall is filled with paintings and decorations, the opposite wall should be open and plain. This creates a balance of Yin and Yang.

The coordination of color and furniture is also important, since with this coordination the qi can link together.

From time to time, we should look at each piece of decoration or furniture, and ask ourselves if it really needs to be there anymore. If it is no longer necessary, we should remove it.

The size of a house has a lot to do with the density of the energy within it. The house provides space for people; the people who live in it provide energy to nourish the house. With the same number of people, a smaller space will have more warmth than a larger one. If the house is too big for the number of people, it doesn't matter how good the decorations or other features are. It will have a tendency to feel cold.

The house should be filled with abundant, healthy houseplants. Houseplants serve as connectors, providers, cleansers, and neutralizers for energy. Most people will have experienced this in public buildings: an abundance of plants makes a space feel much more friendly; a stark place feels cold and even hostile.

An ideal dwelling place always has a balance of Yang and Yin. A house that is too Yang will have Yang problems; a house that is too Yin will have Yin problems. In a house with overabundant Yang energy, with lots of windows providing light and a sense of openness to the outside, it may be easy for the person who lives there to make relationships, yet hard to have stable relationships; she or he may go quickly through one relationship after another. Similarly, if a house is too dark and closed in, there can be stagnation and a lack of connection with the outside, resulting in a lack of any kind of relationship, good or bad.

A Final Checklist

Here is a summary of specific features that are important for romance and relationships.

- The house should have a solid support behind it, presenting a sense of security and making it more relaxed and loving.
- The house should have a wholesome shape, able to provide wholesome energy.
- The energy flow should be smooth and abundant, neither too fast nor too slow. There should not be too many windows—or too few.
- The energy of the house should have a Yin-Yang balance. The main door should be close to the center.
- There should be no conflict in the kitchen. The sink and the stove should not be opposite each other.
- There should be a solid wall behind the bed.
- The bedroom door should be visible from the bed.

- As you sleep in bed, the main entrance should be in front of you, not behind your head (although that entrance is usually not visible when you are in the bedroom).

If these requirements are satisfied, you should not have any problem finding love or romance if you choose to do so. However, the more that are unfulfilled, the more challenges you are likely to have to overcome.

4

Compatibility and Timing

In any human endeavor there are three elements: time, space, and people. In addition to the right place, the right time and the right person are also crucial. In nature, everything has its own time and space. Every plant and animal has its appropriate habitat. Some plants do best in sunlight, others in shade; some animals do well in deserts, others in forests. In the same way, some plants flourish in the summer, while others flourish in the winter. Some animals take over a century to go through their life cycles; others complete the whole cycle in less than a day.

When all the conditions are right, a plant or animal will flourish; otherwise, extra effort is required. If you try to cultivate a tropical plant in a cool zone, even with a lot of extra effort, the results may not be as good as when the plant is growing in its own place. This is true in human affairs as well: people might have excellent qualities in themselves, but may not be readily compatible with each other.

The same thing is true with time: in nature, everything has its own appropriate time. The sun rises and sets; the moon waxes and wanes. When winter passes, spring comes, and seeds start to germinate. Summer is followed by fall and harvest time. When things follow the pattern of the cycle, everything goes well. When something deviates from the natural pattern, consequences ripple throughout the system, not least for the thing that deviated. When flowers bloom too early, a freeze may come and destroy them completely—and also harm the insects involved with them.

Human beings also share these rhythms, and suffer when they deviate from them. These rhythms have been carefully studied in Chinese medicine, and different meridians in the body, and their related organ systems, are said to become active or dominant during different periods of the day. When one's daily cycle is disrupted, the natural flow from the activation of one organ system to another can also be disrupted, causing discomfort or disease. A good example of this is jet lag, which happens when one flies across time zones: one's body is still functioning on the old time while one's surroundings are on a different time.

It is relatively easy to understand these rhythms when we are interested in the best time to eat, or sleep, or work. But dealing with love and romance, it becomes more complicated. These questions often arise: when can I meet my "soul mate"? Is this a good time to get involved in a relationship? How can I know if this is the right person? What traits will my ideal partner or mate possess? All of these questions really boil down to two: the question of the suitable match, and the question of the suitable time.

There are two common approaches to answering these questions: one is essentially mechanical or mathematical; the other is organic. The first leads to an astrological approach; the second requires an inward understanding of the organic rhythms that govern the natural processes of the living universe.

Let's look first at the mathematical and mechanical approach to compatibility—in other words, at astrological approaches.

Compatibility and The Chinese Zodiac

In astrology, both Eastern and Western, there has been extensive discussion about how to find out whether people are compatible, and about how to produce an ideal match.

In China, traditionally, marriage was arranged by the parents, through the help of a matchmaker. When both families, and both individuals, find the general qualifications acceptable, both sides give the birth dates of the prospective couple to a matchmaker, who takes the information to an astrologer, who then checks to see whether the two people are a good match. The information includes the year, the month, the date, and the hour of birth of each member of the couple. These are called the "Four Pillars," and they make up a kind of natal chart. Each pillar is indicated by two Chinese characters, giving a total of eight characters; thus, this is called "Looking at the Eight Characters." If, based on the chart, the astrologer finds that the two people are incompatible, the marriage arrangement is likely to be rejected, no matter how suitable it may otherwise seem. Many tragedies have been created as a result, but people have also argued that even more potential tragedies may have been avoided.

A common, simplified approach is to look only at the birth years of the couple. Since each year is represented by one of the twelve Animal Signs of the Chinese zodiac, the aim is to understand whether the signs of the two people are compatible or not. The twelve Animal Signs are shown in figure 4.1.

There are basically seven types of relationship: two regarded as auspicious or compatible, one regarded as neutral, and four regarded as inauspicious or incompatible. Not good odds!

Type one relationships, the *Triple Harmony* type, are the most compatible. These people are naturally drawn to each other. In these relationships, the signs are 120 degrees apart. People born in the years of the Rat, Dragon, and Monkey are compatible with each other. The years of Ox, Snake, and Rooster are another compatible group, as are Tiger, Horse, and Dog; Rabbit, Sheep, and Pig form the last group.

Type two is the *Mutual Harmony* type. These are compatible, and have a relaxed relationship, but to a lesser degree than the first type. Rat is compatible with Ox; Tiger with Pig; Dog with Rabbit; Rooster with Dragon; Monkey with Snake; and Sheep with Horse.

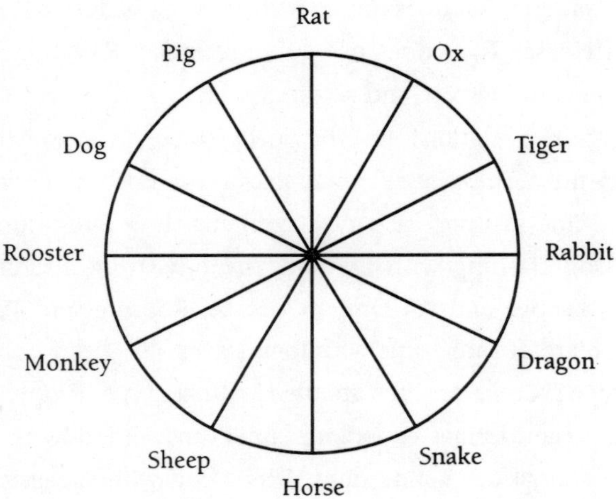

Figure 4.1: Chinese zodiac

Type three relationships are the *Direct Conflict* type. These involve relationships between signs directly opposed to each other (180 degrees apart). Rat and Horse clash; Ox and Sheep clash; Tiger clashes with Monkey; and so on. People in such relationships are naturally opposed to each other; these are the most challenging kind of relationships. People are often advised to avoid such relationships, though from a higher point of view the resulting clashes can provide excellent opportunities for self-discovery and character building.

Type four is the *Indirect Conflict* type. These relationships are moderately challenging, and people in such relationships have to work hard to keep things friendly.

For example, Rat does not go with Sheep; Ox does not go with Horse; Tiger does not go with Snake, Rabbit does not go with Dragon; and so on.

Type five relationships, the *Friction* type, are somewhat unfriendly. These people may get on each other's nerves from time to time. This type contains three subgroups: (a) Dog clashing with Ox and Sheep; (b) Rat clashing with Rabbit; and (c) Dragon, Horse, Rooster, and Pig, which are incompatible with themselves.

Type six relationships are the *Hindrance* type. People in these relationships experience mild ups and downs in somewhat distant connections. This occurs with Rat against Rooster, Ox against Dragon, and Rabbit against Horse.

Type seven, the *Neutral* type, has to do with relationships that do not fall into any of the above six categories. These are often regarded as relatively balanced and friendly relationships. People in such relationships get along, but their connection is easily shaken by small incidents. From a matchmaker's point of view, this is still an acceptable match.

Matchmakers will generally recommend the first two types, Triple Harmony and Mutual Harmony, as favorable matches, and advise against relationships of types three through six.

These seven types of relationship are all summarized in the Chinese Zodiac Relationship Chart in figure 4.2.

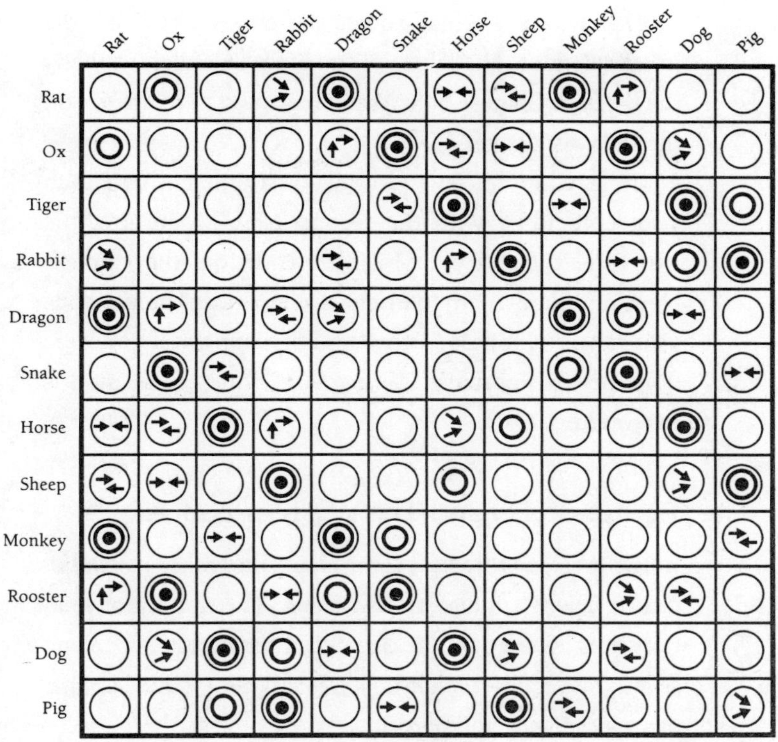

Triple Harmony: The most harmonious and compatible relationship. These people are naturally drawn to each other.

Direct Conflict: Naturally opposed to one another. The most challenging relationship, but a good opportunity for self-discovery.

Mutual Harmony: Comfortable and relaxed relationship. These people are easy and spontaneous together.

Indirect Conflict: Moderately challenging relationship. These people have to work hard to keep things friendly.

Neutral: A balanced and friendly relationship. These people get along, but things are easily shaken by small incidents.

Friction: A somewhat unfriendly relationship. These people may get on each other's nerves from time to time.

Potential: This symbol is not shown in the chart above, but its influence is present in every relationship; represents the potential for people to shape their own destiny.

Hindrance: These people experience mild ups and downs in a somewhat distant connection.

Figure 4.2: Chinese Zodiac Relationship Chart

The Twelve Animal zodiac system is based on the lunar calendar. The tables of the lunar calendar, showing the dates of Chinese New Year, are shown in figure 4.3 on the following page.

(*Note:* Chinese New Year falls on a different date each year, coinciding with the second New Moon after the winter solstice. If your birthday is before the Chinese New Year date in any particular year, count the previous year as your Chinese birth year. For example: if you were born before February 15, in 1961, your zodiac sign is Rat, and not Ox.)

Compatibility and The Western Zodiac

In the West, astrological signs change monthly instead of yearly. There are also twelve signs. The quality of relationships is based on the degrees of separation. There are seven "aspects": *conjunction, semisextile, sextile, square, trine, inconjunct,* and *opposition.*

Conjunction involves no separation; the semisextile, a 30-degree separation; the sextile, a 60-degree separation; the square, a 90-degree separation; the trine, a 120-degree separation; the inconjunct, a 150-degree separation; and the opposition, a 180-degree separation.

In general, conjunction is a powerful relationship, simpatico, in which mutual tendencies are strengthened. It can be harmonious or conflicted, so be sure you are heading in the right direction. Semisextile involves decisions to be made between entirely different people. Relationships can be somewhat stressful, but can provide a

2-10-1910 Dog	2-14-1934 Dog	2-18-1958 Dog	2-25-1982 Dog
1-30-1911 Pig	2-04-1935 Pig	2-08-1959 Pig	2-13-1983 Pig
2-18-1912 Rat	1-24-1936 Rat	1-28-1960 Rat	2-02-1984 Rat
2-06-1913 Ox	2-11-1937 Ox	2-15-1961 Ox	2-20-1985 Ox
1-26-1914 Tiger	1-31-1938 Tiger	2-05-1962 Tiger	2-09-1986 Tiger
2-14-1915 Rabbit	2-19-1939 Rabbit	1-25-1963 Rabbit	1-29-1987 Rabbit
2-03-1916 Dragon	2-08-1940 Dragon	2-13-1964 Dragon	2-17-1988 Dragon
1-27-1917 Snake	1-27-1941 Snake	2-02-1965 Snake	2-06-1989 Snake
2-11-1918 Horse	2-15-1942 Horse	1-21-1966 Horse	1-27-1990 Horse
2-01-1919 Sheep	2-05-1943 Sheep	2-09-1967 Sheep	2-15-1991 Sheep
2-20-1920 Monkey	1-25-1944 Monkey	1-30-1968 Monkey	2-04-1992 Monkey
2-08-1921 Rooster	2-13-1945 Rooster	2-17-1969 Rooster	1-23-1993 Rooster
1-28-1922 Dog	2-02-1946 Dog	2-06-1970 Dog	2-10-1994 Dog
2-16-1923 Pig	1-22-1947 Pig	1-27-1971 Pig	1-31-1995 Pig
2-05-1924 Rat	2-10-1948 Rat	2-15-1972 Rat	2-19-1996 Rat
1-24-1925 Ox	1-29-1949 Ox	2-03-1973 Ox	2-07-1997 Ox
1-02-1926 Tiger	2-17-1950 Tiger	1-23-1974 Tiger	1-28-1998 Tiger
2-02-1927 Rabbit	2-06-1951 Rabbit	2-11-1975 Rabbit	2-16-1999 Rabbit
1-23-1928 Dragon	1-27-1952 Dragon	1-31-1976 Dragon	2-05-2000 Dragon
2-10-1929 Snake	2-14-1953 Snake	2-18-1977 Snake	1-24-2001 Snake
1-30-1930 Horse	2-03-1954 Horse	2-07-1978 Horse	2-12-2002 Horse
2-17-1931 Sheep	1-24-1955 Sheep	1-28-1979 Sheep	2-01-2003 Sheep
2-06-1932 Monkey	2-12-1956 Monkey	2-16-1980 Monkey	1-22-2004 Monkey
1-26-1933 Rooster	1-31-1957 Rooster	2-05-1981 Rooster	1-09-2005 Rooster

Figure 4.3: Chinese New Year 1910–2005 with corresponding animal zodiac sign

new way to see life. Sextile is a harmonious and rewarding relationship, providing opportunities. It is good for creativity, and is regarded as compatible. Square indicates friction between two very different people. It may provide a chance to gain valuable insight and growth, but from a matchmaking point of view it is regarded as undesirable, because the people are not very compatible. Trine is the most compatible and harmonious relationship, but lacks the benefits that come from facing challenges. These people are naturally drawn to each other. Inconjunct involves departure from an accustomed way of being: people in such relationships can be drawn off course. Such relationships are stressful, and require flexibility. Opposition relationships tend to be marked by tension. As with the Chinese astrological configuration involving a 180-degree separation, these relationships are regarded as the least compatible, yet mature people can find in them a powerful balance and heightened awareness.

The Western astrological relationship chart, with traits of the various zodiacal signs, is summarized in figure 4.4 on the following page.

Since Chinese astrological signs focus on the year of birth, and Western astrological signs focus on the month of birth, the combination of the two systems can lead to some interesting insights. For example, if one person is born in the year of the Dragon and one in the year of the Monkey (the most compatible, Triple Harmony type of relationship), and at the same time have Aries and Leo as their sun signs (which are in a Trine relationship, also the most harmonious), this doubling indicates that the relationship should be highly harmonious.

	Aries	Taurus	Gemini	Cancer	Leo	Virgo	Libra	Scorpio	Sagittarius	Capricorn	Aquarius	Pisces
Aries 3/21–4/20	☌	⚺	⚹	■	△	⚻	☍	⚻	△	■	⚹	☌
Taurus 4/21–5/20	⚺	☌	⚺	⚹	■	△	⚻	☍	⚻	△	■	⚹
Gemini 5/21–6/20	⚹	⚺	☌	⚺	⚹	■	△	⚻	☍	⚻	△	■
Cancer 6/21–7/22	■	⚹	⚺	☌	⚺	⚹	■	△	⚻	☍	⚻	△
Leo 7/23–8/22	△	■	⚹	⚺	☌	⚺	⚹	■	△	⚻	☍	⚻
Virgo 8/23–9/22	⚻	△	■	⚹	⚺	☌	⚺	⚹	■	△	⚻	☍
Libra 9/23–10/22	☍	⚻	△	■	⚹	⚺	☌	⚺	⚹	■	△	⚻
Scorpio 10/23–11/21	⚻	☍	⚻	△	■	⚹	⚺	☌	⚺	⚹	■	△
Sagittarius 11/22–12/21	△	⚻	☍	⚻	△	■	⚹	⚺	☌	⚺	⚹	■
Capricorn 12/22–1/19	■	△	⚻	☍	⚻	△	■	⚹	⚺	☌	⚺	⚹
Aquarius 1/20–2/18	⚹	■	△	⚻	☍	⚻	△	■	⚹	⚺	☌	⚺
Pisces 2/19–3/20	☌	⚹	■	△	⚻	☍	⚻	△	■	⚹	⚺	☌

☌ *Conjunction:* Powerful relationship, simpatico, mutual tendencies are strengthened; can be harmonious or conflicted.

⚺ *Semisextile:* Decisions to be made between two entirely different people. Relationship will give these people a new way to see life.

⚹ *Sextile:* Harmonious and rewarding relationship. Provides opportunity; good for creativity.

■ *Square:* Friction between very different people. Provides change to get valuable insight and growth.

△ *Trine:* Most compatible and harmonious relationship, but lack the benefit that comes from facing challenges.

⚻ *Inconjunct:* Departure from an accustomed way of being. Can be drawn off course; relationship requires flexibility.

☍ *Opposition:* May butt heads or be torn apart. Mature people can find a powerful balance and heightened awareness.

⊞ *Potential:* This symbol is not shown in the chart above, but its influence is present in every relationship; represents the potential for people to shape their own destiny.

Figure 4.4: Western Astrological Relationship Chart

What's more, as you can see in the charts, there are additional signs, one in each table, indicating "Potential." These remind us that we do not need to be locked into the astrological formulas. We have the power to choose, and this can lead us to overcome difficulties that might be suggested by an astrological configuration. We have a certain ability to shape the raw materials of our destiny, if we are willing, and able, to do so.

It is easy enough to look at the tables and see whether a relationship is supposed to be compatible or incompatible. But what does this information really mean, and how can it be used? Does being "compatible" necessarily mean that a relationship is good, and being "incompatible" mean that it is bad? To get a sense of how to put this information to use, it is important to examine the whole thing from a higher level, to get the big picture.

Timing and Astrology

The other question is that of timing. How do we know when the time is right to look for a partner, to refrain from looking? How can we tell when the yearning for a relationship will be satisfied, or when the soul mate is most likely to appear? There are extensive discussions, in both Eastern and Western astrology, about ways of judging timing in such matters. In Western astrology, when the moon is in trine with the fifth house, the house of love, it is a good time to fall in love, or to meet people with whom one might fall in love. In Chinese astrology, there are many complex methods. Using the Eight Characters, people can chart out the best times in their lives for meeting compatible people, and also the times they should try to avoid forming relationships. These methods are all quite technical, and require consultation with an experienced professional.

Naturally, there are many other factors that escape the astrological net. Astrological factors can be fun to play with, and may provide some good indications of the factors at work, but they are not the fundamental keys to finding and keeping an appropriate partner.

The Organic Pattern

Astrological approaches have a long history: they appeal to the human desire to know the future. Their knowledge base involves long observation of human affairs, and awareness of statistical patterns. All of these astrological approaches are rather like clock time: they provide a mechanical rhythm against which life is measured. But life operates in terms of organic rhythms that have their own authority, no matter what the clock says. We live our lives in terms of our own feelings and inner processes, and clock time—like astrological calculations—only provides an approximate picture of what is really going on.

Resonance in Love

Compatibility means resonance between two people. In dealing with matters of compatibility, it is most important to realize that a true match must be based on what two people really are. This is why it is useless to try to pretend to be what one is not in order to be compatible with someone else. In such circumstances, even if the pretense works, attracting a person with whom one has no inner resonance is bound to be a frustrating achievement—and may keep away people with whom one is really compatible.

To see in terms of the bigger picture is to see in terms of energy and the rhythms of energy; that is, in terms of organic rather than clock rhythms. These organic rhythms also touch on issues of compatibility and timing.

To be compatible, the energies of two people should synchronize and resonate with each other. It is not uncommon for people to find someone and know, right away, that he or she is the right person. This is the inner aspect of compatibility, which is associated with Yin factors.

A close relationship like this is not a matter of physical proximity, but of energetic resonance, for which distance is no barrier. There is a Chinese saying that goes, "When there is a strong affinity, a thousand miles cannot keep them apart; when there is no affinity, they will not come together even if they live next door."

But compatibility is more than just passion and desire: it also depends on social issues, like family and education, profession and culture. These are not necessarily limiting factors, but they are guiding factors. This is the outer aspect of compatibility, which is associated with Yang factors.

A farm girl who marries into a royal family may make for a good romantic story, but after the initial passion becomes less intense, social compatibility can become an issue. Take a child from a poor rural family, used to scrimping and saving, who marries into a rich family. The traits that were admirably thrifty in one setting can become stingy and miserly in the other. Matches between people of widely different backgrounds can produce good love stories but not necessarily happy families. Passion can start a relationship, but cannot be counted on to sustain it.

The Time Will Come

In human life, in all cultures, there are times for every typical activity: studying, marrying, raising a family, and so on. There are variations in the timing from place to place, but the pattern is still the same.

From very early in human history, people have been pondering how they as individuals fit into these general patterns. From a social (Yang) point of view, there are clearly ideal times to get married, form a family, and raise children. But the question of when to fall in love—the best time to fall in love—is seldom mentioned, since there is a contradiction between the "falling" and any attempts to plan. In other words, love often occurs spontaneously (Yin), and not as a result of manipulations or schemes (Yang).

As in our discussion of compatibility, it is necessary for there to be a balance between the Yang and Yin aspects: neither planning nor spontaneity is sufficient by itself. People often say that timing is everything. To try to dominate a situation by manipulating the timing is a mistake. Do not try to force anything: it is better to yield. Yielding is not the same as giving up; rather, it is a matter of biding one's time, and of sensitivity to the situation. It is a natural, spontaneous process that comes from the clear intuition of a balanced heart. Yielding is not a matter of scheming or planning. Although there are no rules for predicting when the right time comes, we can learn to be sensitive and open so that we can be aware of the changing influences around us.

So we can see that focusing exclusively on the Yin aspect gives initial energy, but may not give sustainability; focusing exclusively on the Yang aspect may be practical, but may also be without initial impetus or inner life. As in all things, both Yin and Yang must exist, and be interacting, for the system to exist as a system—that is, for a relationship to exist and prosper.

If natural processes flow to bring about connections between compatible people, why are so many marriageable people single? The answer is that natural processes are very simple, but human beings have wandered far from natural rhythms; they have interfered with the natural processes that would otherwise bring them together with those who are compatible with them.

Instead of trying to figure out the best time to get involved with someone romantically or otherwise, it might be better to point out the worst time.

The worst time to get into a relationship is when you are absolutely desperate for a relationship. At that time, what you need, what you desire, and what you can offer are not in balance. What you desire may not be what you need, and if you get it things may become even more confusing. You are desperate to fill a hole within you, without having an equal amount to offer in return.

After the end of a long relationship, people will often go through a series of unsatisfying love affairs—or end up making a wrong choice that later has to be undone. On the other hand, when you have absolutely no interest in being in a relationship, it is pretty unlikely that you will end up falling in love.

For people anxiously looking for a better half, the question still remains: when will it happen? The best time is when one naturally falls in love—but how? And when? *All these kinds of questions should be abandoned.*

Anxiety and worry can only inhibit what would otherwise happen. Instead, one should practice confidence that when conditions are right, things will happen. In Yin-Yang Theory, if there is Yin there must be Yang. If there is a lonely heart here, there must be a lonely heart there, as well. The reason you exist in one configuration is that someone else exists in the complementary configuration: Yin and Yang emerge into existence together. If you realize the implications of this, you will have faith that you ultimately cannot be isolated or alone.

As we pointed out in chapter 2, the attraction of Yin and Yang is a natural process: when you are ready, it will come. When you are prepared, it will take place. When you ask, "What can I do to draw someone to me?" the answer is to work on yourself: make your life happy; build your own beacon.

In working on oneself, as in other work, when there are many obstacles, it is better to bide one's time. When there are opportunities, one has to act right away. When resistances are too great, forcing the process will lead to frustration and failure. When the ground is frozen, it is not good to try to plant things. When the ground is warmed up, one has to be ready to plant as soon as possible, to catch the moment. The same thing is true with harvesting: it is useless to try to speed up the harvest. All one can do is be ready, so that when the crop is ripe, one will be able to move immediately to bring it in. In other words, if one prepares one's activities and resources, when the time is right for change, one can mobilize the resources right away, and take full advantage of the opportunity.

In the Tai Chi diagram, when one side is advancing, the other side yields. Yielding does not mean to surrender, but to return at another moment, when the time is right. Therefore, when negative influences are manifesting, do not act, but wait. When positive influences are manifesting, act to catch the time. When opportunity knocks, do not delay, but act quickly to catch the moment.

These are general principles, and may be too abstract to address the anxiety we often feel about when and how to meet the right people—and how to know they are the right ones when we do meet them. Remember the essential point: ultimately, timing and compatibility are not an issue. A compatible match exists; anxiety about arranging one or creating one is a waste of energy and time. When conditions are right, compatible people meet. When they do not meet, it can only be because conditions are not yet right. The answer to the question of why things do not fit with our desires is that, ultimately, in some way we have disrupted or interfered with the natural processes that would have made our world and our desires mesh as one.

Head and Heart

There is a final issue involving compatibility and timing. We have been talking in terms of ideal circumstances. However, in the real world, situations can arise that depart from the ideal.

Sometimes desire arises between two people in circumstances that would make it inappropriate to cross the boundary and act on the desire. Perhaps one (or both) is already married; perhaps they are employer and employee, or student and teacher. How can we deal with such situations? People are often caught between the desire of the heart and the reasoning of the head.

To address this issue, let's return to the fundamentals of Yin and Yang. Surface manifestations (Yang) can be confusing; the solution lies in tracing back to the source, the inner self (Yin). Rather than engaging in judgment and internal debate, people should look into themselves, and try to find the source of this desire or attraction. Is it the result of boredom in the present relationship? Is it a fantasy to counteract despair or unhappiness? Is it a temporary excitement instead of a real love? Is it a matter of a sense of conquest that gratifies ego and pride? Or is it fascination with some quality one has projected onto the other person? Careful self-examination will clarify many such situations; with clarification, many of these situations will dissolve. But there are times when there is a strong desire or attachment that remains, and another aspect of Yin and Yang should be used.

The present is Yang; the future is Yin. In the present, there may be strong fascination and attachment. Try then to visualize life beyond the present, say five or ten years from now. Will he or she be as passionate and as fascinating after five years? After all, five years ago your current relationship was probably much like this one now. Often, when we meet people at work, or in a social situation, we see only an ideal or public person, not the whole person, which includes the private as well as the public. It may well be that, with time and familiarity, the new person might be just as unsatisfactory as one's current partner or mate.

This kind of Yin-Yang analysis will often resolve such problems, putting them into their larger context and showing the origins of the feelings, as long as we can maintain a balanced approach and avoid the temptation to become unbalanced. But there is also the possibility that you find, after careful analysis, that you do have a strong connection with the new person, and truly deep compatibility—and that the current relationship is really not well founded.

There are many circumstances—cultural, religious, legal, and so on—that will have an impact on your decision. All these factors should be considered, but one must also honestly address one's own feelings. If you find, in the end, that you honestly think it is right to make a change, then you should do so. Sometimes people find after a year or two of marriage that they have made a mistake, but take a decade or two to move out of the relationship. This kind of indecision does no service to either party.

Life is magical, and nature is like a magician who may play strange tricks on us, but no matter what the circumstances, life is about the choices we make within the circumstances given to us. What we become arises not from our circumstances, but from the choices we make in dealing with them, and we have to consider, when we choose, what we are choosing to become.

5

Love and Communication

When does a love story have a happy ending? In the West, most of the focus in writing about love is on the first stages: the meeting, courtship, and union of the young couple. But in a real sense this is just the beginning of a long journey. In the East, the standard blessing is, "A hundred years of harmonious unity." Falling in love and getting married is just the beginning, the seedling from which the full relationship grows.

Love Is the Whole Journey

Love is not a prize or a gift, a fruit that falls from the tree. It is a process, the whole life of the tree. Loving relationships, like everything in nature, are dynamic, always moving and changing. If you do not continue to cultivate the tree, it will not grow well, and may not even last long.

To take care of the tree of love is both fulfilling and challenging. No two trees are alike; no two relationships are the same. But their basic requirements are the same: devotion, patience, sensitivity, and awareness. Different trees may require different soil, water, light, and temperature. Some trees are known for their blossoms, some for their fruits, and some for their overall beauty. Also, different stages in the growing process require different kinds of attention. To take care of a tree when it is a seedling is different from taking care of it when it is mature. You have to be sensitive to its own life cycle: you cannot speed up or delay the process. If the tree naturally blossoms in the late spring, it is not good to try to push it to blossom in the early spring. If you prune it at the wrong time, the tree might become distorted or misshapen.

The same thing is true with cultivating, maintaining, and enhancing a relationship. In general, there is the greatest excitement in the earlier stages of a relationship. After the relationship stabilizes, or after getting married, things seem to change, even to become boring. This is why people sometimes say that "marriage is the prison of love." But in fact, it is the beginning of a long journey.

A long journey is just like a river: it begins with a few small springs merging into a larger stream, comes to a waterfall or rapids, then drops through mountainous terrain to the plains, and eventually runs to the sea. Marriage is the mountain stream right after the thunder of the waterfall. Once past the rapids or waterfall, the stream has a different kind of beauty. It may still run through many different kinds of terrain, twisting and turning as it goes, faster and slower at various times, sometimes singing like a flock of birds returning to the forest in the evenings, or thundering like a wild horse galloping across an open field. When the river finally reaches the plains, it becomes peaceful and quiet.

The beauty of this long journey, once the falls are passed, provides even more inner fulfillment and joy. But people are often stuck on the stage of the thundering waterfall, of passionate intensity, as if that were the whole picture. If there is a waterfall, there must be a river afterward; if there is Yang, there must also be Yin—and a transition from the dynamic Yang stage to the peaceful Yin stage. When the stream has just emerged and is roaring through the mountains, it is natural that it will be dynamic and exciting; when it reaches the plains, it will be naturally peaceful and stable.

It is human nature or habit to focus on a particular moment, to focus on only one stage of the journey, and miss the river as a whole. Both dynamic and peaceful phases have their own beauty. People often mistakenly see the difference between the intensity of courtship and the relative quiet after marriage as a shift from one relationship to another. It seems that the first relationship has ended, and been replaced by another—one that is less exciting, and one that requires less attention and cultivation. This also involves mistakenly breaking a continuous sequence into rigid phases. But the river flows as a whole, not as a collection of segments contained in the boundaries drawn on a map. When we expand our perspective, we can enjoy the whole journey by seeing the whole picture. The right perspective (to see the story of love in terms of the full course of the journey) and the right attitude (to see every stage as involving mutual curiosity and mutual discovery, at a slower but deeper pace) form a good foundation of a lasting and rewarding relationship.

However, any loving relationship involving two souls is always dynamic and challenging. How well the Yin and Yang energies merge together depends on the quality of communication that occurs between them. Good communication plays an important role in every stage of human love affairs. Often enough, the right people who meet at the right time do not get together because of miscommunication—or people may pick up the wrong signals and invest a lot of energy only to get negative results.

The right perspective and the right attitude are important, but good communication is crucial. Good communication is a key element in courtship: a well-matched couple may break apart through miscommunication, or a poorly matched couple may struggle fruitlessly to stay together because they do not have a clear understanding of their incompatibilities.

The Secret of Communication

We often think of communication as an exchange of ideas, thoughts, or desires between or among people. We think of it occurring through physical means: written or spoken words, or gestures. But in reality, the human body, like the universe and everything in it, is an open system. It never stops emitting, receiving, and exchanging energy and information with what is around it. In a general sense, we are constantly communicating with everything around us—and, in fact, through our connection with the cosmos, with everything in it.

Although in practical terms we think of communication as being an exchange with intentional targets, we cannot neglect the fact that it actually occurs over a very broad range, whether or not we intend for it to occur.

Many people do not fully understand how communication actually works; even less, that it is possible to work with patterns of communication just as one works with other natural patterns, like the flow of water or air.

In any communication, information flows in all directions at once. There are always Yin (unconscious) and Yang (conscious) aspects. The Yang aspect of communication is the one that clearly manifests through voice and gesture, at a conscious level. The Yin aspect of communication deals with the unseen or unconscious level of communication. Of course, most communication of which we are aware belongs to the first pattern: it is verbal, enhanced by bodily gestures. However, when one speaks, as one projects on a conscious level, one also projects on an unconscious level. Sometimes the other person is able to pick up on the unconscious communication, and sometimes not.

If two people are talking, we can say that there are four channels of communication between them (see figure 5.1).

The first channel involves conscious to conscious (Yang-Yang) communication. One person consciously says something, and the other person is aware of what is being said.

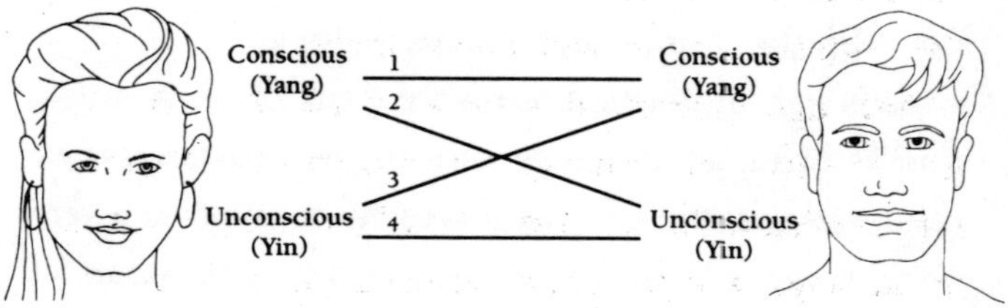

Figure 5.1: Four channels of communication

The second channel involves conscious communication by one person, but unconscious perception by the other, who may feel that something is going on, without being able to catch on to what it is. This is the Yang to Yin channel.

The third channel involves an unconscious expression that is perceived consciously by the second person, who realizes that the first person has expressed something without being aware of it, or without intending to express it. This is the Yin to Yang channel.

The fourth channel is where both expression and perception are unconscious (the Yin to Yin channel). Neither party is explicitly aware of what is being communicated, but it nevertheless has effects. An unconscious thought-form may be projected by one person and received by another without passing through awareness on either side. This kind of information can still affect people, even if they do not react right away. But in this kind of communication, people don't know why they are reacting as they do.

Often people do not fully speak what is in their hearts, and they assume that because they have not expressed their thoughts verbally (or through some other means, like gestures), other parties will not pick up on it. But this is not the case.

People do pick up nonverbal, implicit communications. This is why salespeople who believe in the value of their products can project their confidence and make sales without much effort. If salespeople are not sure about their product, then no matter how smooth the verbal presentation, the buyer may hesitate, since buyers may pick up the nonverbal thoughtform through Yin to Yang communication.

In any communication, all these patterns happen simultaneously, at different strengths. This is why attempts to cheat or manipulate people through verbal communication are so often futile. You may feel that what you are saying is reasonable, yet people aren't accepting it. This is because they are picking up on contradictory information that you are conveying subconsciously.

People have, unfortunately, gotten into the habit of going through many futile processes in an attempt to manipulate communications. However, the truth is that the more one attempts to manipulate communications, the more people become aware of those attempts, and the less the attempts work.

This is why openness and truthfulness are naturally the best way to communicate. The universe is an open system: nothing can ever be hidden.

In fully open and truthful communication, all four patterns of communication are unified: nothing is hidden, and there is no distinction between conscious and unconscious. People waste a great deal of energy trying to outplay each other in different kinds of communication games. Without these efforts, life would be much simpler.

The First Communication

Truthful communication is vital. However, people are often not clear about what they are really wanting, thinking, or feeling. When one is not clear about what one wants, thinks, or feels, one can hardly communicate it clearly to others.

The first and most important kind of communication is communication with, and within, one's self. Self-communication means fully understanding oneself. Only with a full understanding of oneself can one carry on undistorted communication with others. It is not unusual for one person to talk for hours with someone only to have the listener eventually say, "I really don't know what you want." This often happens when the person who is talking doesn't know what he or she wants either.

Clear self-communication, which forms the foundation for all other kinds of communication, comes from a process of self-awareness. Only with very clear self-communication can we begin to clarify issues that arise when we engage in targeted communication with others. To understand others, one must first understand oneself.

The Yin and Yang of Communication

Communication involves transmitting and receiving, which we can call the Yang and Yin aspects, respectively. If the receiver is not functioning well, then no matter how strong the transmitter, the message will not be getting through. Similarly, no matter how good the receiver, if the transmitter is not functioning, then no messages will be delivered.

People often think that others will receive their message as soon as they speak. This is why people so often say such things as "How many times do I have to tell you . . ." or "I've already told you many times . . ."

Female and male, as representatives of Yin and Yang, have different characteristic energies; their ways of transmitting and receiving are also different. Women may not be as straightforward as men in transmitting their ideas; men are not always effective listeners, or good at playing the receiving role.

It is always important to be aware of the inherent nature of these Yin and Yang differences in dealing with communication issues. This applies to both the message itself and to the participants in the exchange.

Getting the Message Through

Being open and truthful, and clear within oneself, is one thing; how one communicates or transfers the information, however, is often a different matter.

In any relationship, there are bound to be things that one likes and things that one dislikes. It is important, and not difficult, to communicate clearly what one enjoys, or finds agreeable. The problem comes when there are things one dislikes, or about which there is disagreement.

Some unpleasant things may not be particularly important—but it is important to recognize clearly what they are, and to see that they are in fact unimportant. Without this recognition, one is likely to unconsciously project low levels of annoyance whenever such issues arise. If, on the other hand, one fully recognizes them as unimportant, one will project clarity and acceptance instead of unconscious annoyance.

Of course, there are also times when one really needs to communicate clearly about serious difficulties. Lovers often try to come up with schemes and strategies for getting this sort of message through. All game plans or strategies might work, and you may achieve limited goals for a limited time, but not without a price.

If you dislike something that someone does, you may try to keep the feeling inside—but since there is no inside (because the human organism is an open system), this effort will not succeed. At the same time, this does not mean that you must deliver the information as forcefully and directly as possible. A curved line is often better than a straight line. Remember: the patterns of nature are circular, not linear. It is easy to fill a container of water in a gentle stream; it is much harder to do so in a raging river. Information delivered in an abrupt and forceful way may not get through; the intended recipient may be put off by the delivery, and so will resist noticing the content. Or the message may get through, but it will bounce off without leaving an impression. The same information, delivered gently, may arrive before anyone thinks to resist it. But a curved line is not a twisted line: the message, though gently delivered, should be clear.

This is just a general guideline. Delivering messages is an art that improves with practice and experience, and much depends on the two people involved. Careful attention will always improve one's skills.

The Right Time to Deliver—and Respond

In dealing with relationships, from newly formed ones to old, long-lasting ones, the key is to follow natural rhythms. Clear communication is important, as is the delivery of a message. But *when* to deliver it—the question of timing—is just as important.

Human beings are rhythmic animals, and human emotions manifest in different temporal patterns. It is important to understand those patterns, and find the best times for both projection and reception. When one side is not in a receiving mode, it is a waste of time and energy for the other to project.

When one is Yang, the other should be Yin: when one is talking, the other ideally should be listening. When one is projecting frustration and anger as Yang, it is often better if the other does not respond in the same way. Yang to Yang does not work: when one pushes, the other should yield. To yield is not to be destroyed; to yield is to transform opposing energy and maintain one's own balance.

Take a young professional couple who both work full-time. When the husband has had a long day, comes home tired and frustrated, and finds that the house is messy, or dinner is not ready, his irritation might focus on his wife. The wife could resist and return the anger at the same time, with the result that the two angers would confront each other. On the other hand, if the wife can neutralize the husband's anger at this point, a long evening of recriminations can be avoided. Then, after dinner, when the husband has calmed down, the wife can point out the irrationality and unfairness of his expectations—and he will be much more likely to hear and accept what she has to say. This may also be the time for the wife to pull out her own issues, and place them on the table for consideration.

In the Tai Chi diagram, the boundary that connects Yin and Yang is a curved line, not a straight line. In other words, when Yang pushes, it is yielding that gives Yin momentum to push back.

A good relationship can be measured by the fulfillment of expectation and desire. Human emotions are so complex that people often avoid putting them into words. They don't want to lose the power and magic of their emotions. This is why people often do not wish to say what they really want. To have an unspoken desire fulfilled is very different from having a spoken request fulfilled. Love means that you do not have to say a lot.

Truthful communication, the right way to transmit it, and the right time to transmit it, are the essential aspects of cultivating a good relationship. It is impossible to overemphasize the power of truthfulness. True words have power: they penetrate to the depths of the soul. As we grow up, we learn to give speeches like politicians, relying on technique to get our messages across. However, politicians, like actors, need technique because they are often simulating the truth, rather than speaking the truth. But truth has its own energy.

The Magic of Whispering

We often think that strong delivery will help to get a message across. But in a very real sense, a soft, even whisper-like delivery, which is Yin, will tend to resonate more with the receiving entity, which in receiving is also Yin. This is why in many situations it is better to whisper. Whispering has a special magic. Often schoolteachers who have a hard time controlling a rowdy class can get better results when they whisper than they can when they shout. All the students become quiet because they want to hear the secret.

Human nature has a tendency to underestimate the power of Yin, of nonmanifestation, of subtlety. Projection, manifestation, and delivery have to do with the Yang or masculine force. But Yin is a power as real as Yang. A quiet voice, a soft touch, a light thought, or a vague image can be more effective than their Yang equivalents. If you hold a pebble with a strong grip, all you can feel is the tension in your muscles. Only if you hold it lightly can you feel the texture and quality of the stone itself. The same thing is true for all our senses, all our avenues of perception. Strong projection can provoke resistance, and the receiver primarily experiences the rigidity of resistance; gentle projection creates attention, and then the receiver can attend to what is being communicated.

Communicating at the right time, in the right way, will help to provide a good basis for a good relationship. However, despite all good intentions, there is often another issue: that of perception.

The different energy patterns characteristic of male and female lead to different ways of perceiving situations, and lead to different perspectives on the human world. This often leads to a gap between the male and female perception of a situation.

Often a woman will perceive issues or problems in a relationship that the man does not recognize or even perceive. Regardless of whether the problem or issue is "real" or not, when one person perceives the existence of a problem and the other does not, there is a very real problem between them. This is why it is crucial for men to be sensitive and to pay attention when such issues arise. This requires the right attitude, the willingness to pay attention, and awareness and sensitivity—the *capacity* to pay attention.

To do this requires intuition. Some people are naturally more intuitive than others. But how can we develop this kind of awareness and sensitivity? How can we sharpen our intuition? Sensitivity comes more easily when body and mind are relaxed, and when the heart is open. Intuition, however, requires going a step further.

Cultivating Intuition

What exactly is intuition? How can it be defined? Is it a gut feeling? Is it what you just know, for no particular reason? If we follow our intuition, we suppose that we cannot make mistakes, since intuitive energy is the natural energy of the cosmos. Often, however, we think we are following our intuitions—but we bump our heads. "I just feel that he (or she) is a good person, and is the right one for me." And then, a few weeks later, "What a mistake!"

How can gut feelings go so wrong? If it were indeed a real intuition, it would not go wrong. What then is real intuition? Intuition is a feeling—the *very first* feeling, the *very first* thought. But in a split second, a dozen thoughts can already pass through our minds: it is not always easy to catch the very first one.

When someone hands you a beautiful rose, you are generally hardly aware of your first feeling, because you immediately recognize that it is a rose, that it is red; you catch its scent, and you start to think about what it could mean. The very first thought has long gone, before you are even aware of what it was.

How then can we catch these very first thoughts? How can we develop intuition? People may think that the way to do this is through meditation, energy work, and so on. These help, somewhat, but the idea of learning and practicing such methods may be misleading because it implies that it can take years of special effort to develop any real intuition.

The natural way is the simple way, one that uses something we already have and already use. To develop intuition is to begin following your feelings. The feelings that you follow may not be the first ones that arise, and this may lead you to bump your head from time to time. But your feelings are the vehicle you already have. The important thing is that, even if you bump your head many times, do not be frustrated or resentful. It is this response of frustration that leads people to shut down their own inner knowledge and rely only on what other people tell them. Instead, simply acknowledge to yourself that you must have missed the initial feeling, and continue to pay attention, and to trust your sense of your first feeling the next time around.

As you continue to trust your feelings, the feelings you notice will come closer and closer to the initial thought or feeling. You will gradually find that you are catching the right feeling, and you will reach the stage in which you feel comfortable that what you know is true. Do not give up on yourself. Remember that you are nature; you are the universe; you are the energy of the cosmos.

Sensitivity, awareness, and intuitive understanding of each other will profoundly enrich any relationship. It is not difficult to cultivate these traits; it is crucial not to overlook them. Many relationships between people who are otherwise very compatible have been seriously damaged by a lack of attention to these matters.

One of the most fulfilling events is having someone respond to you without being told what to do. Even more rewarding, however, is being able to respond to another without needing to be told what to do. This leads to a realization of connection at a very deep level, one that goes far beyond the ordinary conscious world.

In all, to have the right perspective on the long journey of love, to have the right attitude of continuous searching and discovery even after two hearts have become one, and to have clear and good communication—this will ensure a truly beautiful love story.

6

Body, Mind, and Qi

"It must take a lot of energy to raise a baby," said a man to a young mother who was busy with her baby. "No," she answered, "it doesn't take energy, it just takes love."

This must have been her first baby. If it were her second or third, she would have realized that love has to come from somewhere. Love is one manifestation of qi. This particular manifestation rests on two pillars: the body and the mind. Without physical strength and energy, and without the proper emotional balance, love is simply a cloud in a sunny sky, not able to manifest as rain.

It doesn't matter whether it's a young couple just entering the romance of love, or an old couple with a well-seasoned relationship—a healthy body and balanced mind are key ingredients for any relationship to be solid and fulfilling. (This is not to say that these two ingredients are sufficient for romance—but they certainly are necessary.) A healthy body and healthy mind lead to flourishing love.

There are many ways to look at the issue of health, and many ways to work with it. What is a healthy body? Doctors can provide a long list of parameters to determine how healthy you are: pulse rate, blood pressure, cholesterol profile, and so on. On the other hand, a health club trainer might use a very different set of parameters to determine how healthy you are. But no one set of parameters gives the whole picture: none provides a definitive picture of your health.

Of course, in general terms a healthy body is one that can function well in daily life: eating well, sleeping well, thinking well, working well, and loving well.

Another way to look at health is to look at the level of energy: to examine how abundant the qi is. The abundance of qi is like a summary indicator for all sets of parameters. Where there is abundant qi, there is abundant life and abundant health. Unfortunately, we are not able to quantify qi—we have to rely on judging the quality of its manifestations.

One of the most important ways of improving health, and enhancing the flow of qi, is exercise. There is a Chinese saying—"Flowing water does not stagnate"—that is often taken to describe the value of activity in keeping the body healthy.

When people think of exercise, they often think of playing sports such as basketball, softball, or soccer, or working out at a health club, using exercise machines and gadgets. There are many options; each is good in its own way, and each fits into a particular purpose and lifestyle. Sports exercises are mostly beneficial for the muscular and cardiovascular systems; they enhance metabolism, reduce the burden on the heart, and lower cholesterol levels. For the past few decades, many health professionals have jumped on the bandwagon of jogging and running. While jogging and running are natural for four-legged animals like dogs and horses, for human beings walking is more natural.

Today there are a great many fitness programs and exercises that rely on tools and gadgets. All claim to have great results. Exercise gadgets tend to be most appealing to people who want shapely bodies—slender and light, or strongly muscled and powerful.

However, all of the aforementioned options have serious limitations, and they are not necessarily directly linked to health promotion. Athletes and sports stars do not, statistically, live longer than average. Jim Fixx, a long-time promoter of jogging in the United States, had a heart attack at a relatively young age.

When people get sick, or cannot perform adequately, it is often not because their muscles are weak or their bodies aren't shapely. Sickness generally comes from dysfunction of internal organ systems: kidney failure, heart failure, and so on. The Western approach to health is very different from that in Asia. It is important to remember that modern medicine is at most a century or so old—unlike the medical traditions of China and India, which go back for thousands of years. Western medicine has done great things in eradicating bacterial and viral diseases, and in developing sophisticated diagnostic tools, but in dealing with functional health problems and diseases it is still in its early stages. Traditional medicine in Asia has long recognized the complex energy system of the body, and has developed a sophisticated theory to explain it. Many of the traditional exercises in Asia address the issue of strengthening internal organs and balancing energy, rather than focusing on the external musculature.

The natural way is the simple way—this is one of the basic principles that can guide us. People tend to look for answers outside themselves, and from exotic places. Relying on exercise machines and gadgets, letting them tell us how much work we are doing, how fast we are walking, and how much we are lifting, is a manifestation of this tendency.

Any ideal exercise or health-promotion method should be natural and simple, and possible to implement in your daily life without much extra effort. It should not require a special place, or special tools or gadgets. There are many ordinary, easy ways to promote health that do not require joining a gym or health club.

Let's begin with something very simple and close to us.

Abdominal Breathing

Health issues are really qi issues. And one of the most important aspects of dealing with qi is the breath. There are many traditions that use breathing as a way to promote energy and health. Each one has its own special methods.

Of all these methods, abdominal breathing is one of the most direct, and it is simple to work with in one's daily life. When you breathe abdominally, your belly extends outward when you inhale and returns inward when you exhale. When first practicing this, you can put your hands on your belly to help become aware of how your belly pushes out when you inhale and pulls in when you exhale. If you do this exercise correctly, when you place both palms over your kidneys (on your back, the soft space between the lowest ribs and the top of the pelvis), as you inhale you can feel the two kidneys being pushed outward. (This is just an indicator to show the effectiveness of the exercise—the health benefits don't depend on how far you can push your kidneys!) After practicing for a while, your breathing pattern gradually becomes longer: the inhalations and exhalations become deeper. As you become comfortable with this, you can add a period of pause between inhalation and exhalation and prolong the breathing cycle. At the beginning, this may require a little deliberate effort, but it is not something you should overdo or force.

Why does abdominal breathing benefit the health? The horizontal motion of the abdomen tends to create motion within the organs, especially the kidneys, stomach, and liver. People sometimes call this "internal massage," or massage for the internal organs. The center of the abdomen is the center of power, the basis of energy. By working with it, we awaken energy and activate the qi.

Abdominal breathing is very simple, yet very beneficial. It can be done at any time, for any length of time, whenever you remember to do so. Gradually, it becomes a natural pattern. This method can also be used to prevent sickness. If you are caught in rain and wind, and think you might catch cold, calm down and do this breathing exercise. If you can perform the exercise for even ten minutes, you will be able to ward off the threatening cold, or at least reduce its effects.

Washing Dishes and Cleaning the House

Since childhood, we have been programmed to see washing the dishes and cleaning the house as "work," and to see sports as "exercise" and "play." But they are both movement. Why don't people at the gym see what they are doing as work? Why can't we see household activities as exercise or play?

Household activities are, in fact, great exercise. Instead of going to the gym to "work out" for a couple of hours, people could stay at home and "work in," "exercising" around the house.

This can also be a very powerful spiritual practice. When you are washing dishes or cleaning cups, try to visualize something further: imagine that you are cleansing your body. As you remove dirt from the carpet, you are cleansing your mind. As the dishes are cleaned, the body is cleansed, step-by-step. As the house is cleaned, the mind and emotions are purified.

Whether housework is a nuisance or a powerful cleansing process is determined by a simple flip of one's thoughts. This is an especially good exercise for men, since the kitchen is often viewed as women's territory. The more a man spends time and energy in the kitchen, the more his energy will merge with that of the woman who also spends time there, and the more this will contribute to the engagement of their male and female energies.

How wonderful this exercise is! Cleaning the kitchen and house automatically cleanses your body, calms your emotions, and brings peace to your mind—and your partner appreciates you all the more. Naturally, this will enhance your romantic relationship.

Working In the Yard and Garden

Working in the yard or garden involves more movement than housework, and consumes or uses more energy—but you are in touch with the earth, and with living things. This connection will automatically energize your qi. When you work with the land and with living plants, try to visualize that each one you are working with is also a person: in fact, you are doing a special kind of dance with the plants.

People who work in an office for long hours not only get physically tired, but also emotionally stressed. But for people who work in a garden, even physical tiredness does not translate into emotional distress. This is why it is so crucial to have a connection to the earth, and to the life forces within it. This naturally brings your body into good shape.

A beautiful garden or environment, an energized body, and peaceful emotions—any exercise that produces these things is a great exercise. People who live in apartments, or who don't have a yard or garden, can take care of houseplants, especially plants that require such routine attentions as watering and repotting. This gives people greater contact with the earth, which is very important for those who are otherwise cut off from it.

Breathing, washing dishes and cleaning the house, and gardening: these three things are all easy to implement in our daily lives. They do not require any special effort. Special effort comes from human ideas, not from natural law.

Walking, Playing, and Dancing

Walking, playing, and dancing lead us beyond the scope of our daily lives. Walking is far better than jogging or running: jogging can involve a more fixed pattern of activity, and thus may tend to cultivate inflexibility rather than flexibility. Excessively stressful exercise tends to create a burden on the heart, and may even accelerate the aging process. If you do need more of a cardiovascular workout, you can walk quickly, choose a route with varying elevations, or increase the length of your walk.

Playing is always wonderful: with a partner, with groups, with animals or pets. In play, all parts of the physical body are used, in all sorts of ways, and there is always an element of flexibility and surprise. Play is natural: all children and animals play, and play is the language through which they communicate. There is no reason for adults not to play. Play is a process that links people and energy together.

Dance, from formal to informal, can be seen as a special kind of play. There are several kinds of dances, from easy to very strenuous; however, they all share a close involvement with rhythm and pattern that can be very helpful in integrating physical and mental energies.

With these four groups of exercise, people should find themselves in good health, in improved physical condition, and much more able to enjoy themselves and each other. This is usually enough. Of course, people sometimes want to go the extra mile. When this is the case, one can take up sports.

Sports are organized play. They have social benefits, like teaching teamwork and coordination, as well as physical and emotional benefits. But for health purposes, they are still second to such things as yoga, Tai Chi, and Qi Gong.

There is nothing wrong with working out in a health club or gym. But remember to follow the natural sequence: from inside to outside, from immediate to less immediate. Do your abdominal breathing exercises before any session of sports activity. And before you go to the gym, make sure the dishes are clean, and the houseplants and garden are healthy and well cared for.

Good exercise gives us a basis for healthy physical function. But since body and mind are two sides of one coin, it also leads to healthier and better-balanced emotional states, which are very important for developing and maintaining healthy relationships. When emotions are unhealthy and unbalanced, they can be disruptive and inharmonious, and can easily get us into trouble. When they are healthy and balanced, it is much easier to work with them in a mindful way.

Mindful Relationships

"He has a sense of humor." "He's gentle and kind." "He's reliable and trustworthy." "He's fun." "She's sensitive." "She's strong, and has a great personality." "She's tender and understanding."

Besides beauty and occupation, these are the kinds of qualities men and women often cite when describing their lovers, or why they have chosen them. People often summarize this as "good chemistry."

The fundamental prerequisite, though, is still a balanced heart and mind. It is important for people to love themselves, to be self-confident, and to enjoy being with themselves.

Love is not just a box of chocolates, sweet and tasty. For human beings, there are thousands of emotions beyond the basic opposites of laughing and crying. Energy flows in the mental and emotional worlds just as much as it does in the physical world. The question is how to deal with this movement of energy within oneself.

Emotions are a fundamental psychological process: they occur at many levels and scales. Some emotions, like hope, satisfaction, joy, and so on, allow energy to flow freely. Other emotions, however, like guilt, sorrow, or anger, block energy flow, and even seem to weaken us by draining energy. These unbalanced energies play an important role in hindering or damaging relationships, and can have real destructive effects.

Some damaging emotions are simple; others are more complex. The basic, unmixed damaging emotions are traditionally said to be anger, mania, worry, sorrow, and fear. Mixed with attachments, misunderstandings, and misperceptions, they become such complex feelings as greed, arrogance, jealously, spite, malice, and so on.

All such emotions drain energy or block energy flow, and consequently affect health and relationships. To deal with these emotions is to accept that they are something we must learn to deal with, and to let go.

The very first step is to be aware; the second is to accept and acknowledge; the third is to pay attention and watch, to analyze and understand. This might be far easier to say than to do. However, if one begins with the first step and goes from there, it is not hard to do. In a real sense, one comes to see that such emotions are illusions: they do not have any real substance of their own, but are just conglomerations of reactions. As one sees such a tangle of feelings more and more clearly, one can simultaneously disentangle the feelings, and they fade away like mist in strong sunlight.

Any good relationship with others begins with oneself. Only when one is balanced within can one have a good relationship with others. *In searching for an external balance of Yin and Yang, one must first have an internal balance of Yin and Yang.* Only when one can love oneself can one love a partner or other people. It is therefore crucial that people can find balance and happiness within themselves. However, as the Bible says, we come into this world with a burden of sin; or, as Buddhists say, we come to the world to work out our karma. Imbalance comes along with being born: a balanced mind doesn't come naturally, but takes work. We have to cope with entanglements, and learn how to deal with them more effectively, by seeing them clearly.

Often, when people argue, one will say to the other, "Don't get angry at me," and the other will yell back, "I'm not angry!" This is an example of how people are often not aware of their own emotional states. Even when it is pointed out, it is not easy to acknowledge. Only when people become aware of, and are able to acknowledge, their own emotional states, are they able to pay attention to their thought processes. Just by doing so, one gradually comes to see that such emotional states have no benefits and many costs; at that point, one becomes ready to let the disturbed emotional states go, one by one.

The fundamental emotions arise in the response of our six senses to information from the outside. Information comes in; emotion flows out. The emotions cannot be hidden; one cannot pretend they are not there. Many people become sick because they receive bad energy and hold on to their response to it. This can plant the seed of cancer or other sicknesses. Emotion should be allowed to flow through; but just allowing it to flow is not enough. There must be attention and awareness. Without attention and awareness, there will only be repetition, either of holding or of releasing. We have emotions like anger or fear for a reason. With awareness, we can see these causes, and deal with our relationship to them.

In the Buddhist understanding, all suffering comes from attachment, and attachment comes from the ignorance that keeps one from seeing the reality of things. The best thing is to be able to see through the knot of ignorance and attachment, and thus untie it. Even if one cannot see through the situations that lead to emotional imbalance, as long as one can see the imbalance at all, one can begin to deal with it. There are methods for doing so that do not require the higher level insight that dissolves the problems completely.

Emotions Are Not Just Psychological

The body and the mind are closely related. The mental processes consume energy, and can easily have effects on health. The ancient Chinese medical classic, *The Yellow Emperor's Classic of Internal Medicine,* written two thousand years ago, already had a great deal of information on how the mind affects the body.

Emotional problems are not simply psychological—they derive from physiology as well as psychology. In other words, they don't just come from the head; they come from the rest of the body as well. A weekly visit to a psychotherapist is one way to deal with emotional problems—but not the only way, nor always the best way, since, by seeing a psychotherapist, a problem that arises from a physiological situation can be missed. For example, when someone is easily irritated, this might be due to a weakness in what Chinese medicine calls the liver system. This is why paying attention to, and caring for, the liver system can help ease such problems. In the same way, people who overindulge in worries may have a problem connected with the digestive system, and it may be that the key is to work with the digestive system rather than the worries themselves.

Western medicine, though it has become more aware of the connections between emotions and health, still focuses largely on the general mental and emotional state, without looking at consistent patterns of interrelationship between specific bodily functions and specific types of emotion. Chinese medicine has been aware of the relationship between emotions and health for thousands of years, and has linked specific emotional states with specific disruptions of bodily processes. The five fundamental negative emotions (anger, mania, worry, sorrow, fear) have a very interesting relationship, one that is illustrated by Five Element Theory. Because these emotions correspond to the elements, they can be controlled in the same way that other things corresponding to the elements can be controlled.

As we can see from table 6.1, each of the elements is linked to a specific emotion, organ, and sound.

Element	Emotion	Organ	Sound
Wood	Anger	Liver	Xu
Fire	Mania	Heart	Ke
Earth	Worry	Spleen	Hu
Metal	Sorrow	Lung	Si
Water	Fear	Kidney	Cui

Figure 6.1: Five Element Theory table: Elements, Emotions, Organs, and Sound

If we look at how emotions transform, anger leads to mania, mania to worry, worry to sorrow, and sorrow to fear, which leads back to anger. This relationship goes clockwise around the outside of the circle, as shown in figure 6.2 (page 124). The dotted lines show the controlling or restrictive relationship. For example, anger and worry do not coexist; being manic and mournful does not coexist, and so on.

Things in the same category resonate with each other: emotions, therefore, are linked with associated organs. Anger affects the liver, which is in charge of the qi flow; at the same time, liver disruptions can lead to irritability. Worry interacts with digestion. Sorrow interacts with breathing. Fear interacts with the kidney functions. Any technique that affects the organs can also affect the emotions, and vice versa.

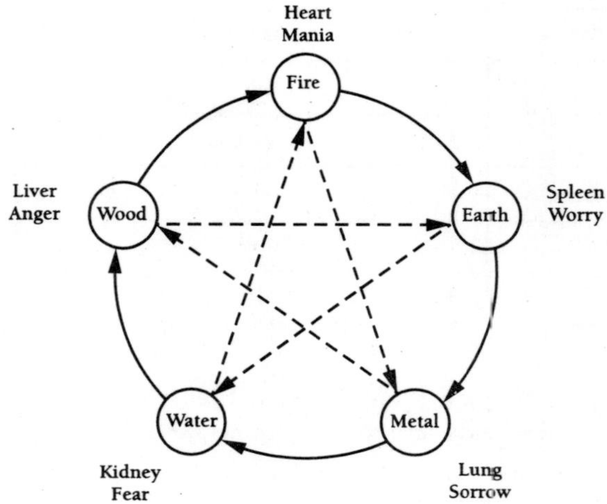

Figure 6.2: Transformation of the elements and emotions

The Five Healing Sounds

Five Sound Therapy is a simple method of dealing with emotions and health, and has been used in China for centuries. By pronouncing each of five different sounds, one can create different vibrations that resonate with specific organs and their emotions. (The sounds written in table 6.1 are spelled in the standard Chinese roman letter writing system. It is not always easy to see the pronunciation from the spelling, so detailed instructions on pronunciation follow.)

To smooth liver qi or calm anger, use the sound "xu." The vowel part of this sound is made with the lips rounded while trying to make an "eee" sound. The "x" part is actually like an English "sh" sound, but with the tongue forward near the teeth.

To cool down manic or overexcited states, and calm and nourish the heart, use a "ke" sound. This sounds like "cub" without the "b" at the end.

To erase worries and help the digestive system, use a "hu" sound. This is pretty much like the word "who," but with the vowel extended.

To relieve sorrow, and to enhance lung function, use the sound "si," made with the mouth open, rather like the word "sir" without the "r" at the end.

To alleviate fear and aid the kidney system, use the sound "cui," which rhymes with "sway," but begins with a "ts" sound instead of just an "s" sound.

These sounds have been used in the Chinese medical tradition for thousands of years, and have proved very effective. (However, in the Taoist tradition one more sound is used, "xi," which rhymes with "she"; the "sh," however, is more like the "tion" in "expedition" than the "sh" in "shun" or "shirt.")

To deal with a particular emotion, you can choose the corresponding sound and repeat it thirty-six times. For general energy balancing and enhancement, practice all of them in sequence, pronouncing each one six times.

This may seem very simple, but it works, and has worked for thousands of years. Many people find that the best time to practice this is while taking a shower. Since water is a sacred substance, and a good medium, allow it to create a resonance. This does not take much effort, and it produces excellent results, which should be noticeable within a few weeks. Effective natural processes are always simple, and are always close at hand.

Couples can use these sounds to help balance their relationship and build rapport. After going through the entire cycle several times, a special quality of feeling will be created.

Emotions in Relationship

In any romantic relationship one must be able to deal with one's own emotions *and* with one's partner's emotions as part of handling the relationship.

This is not complicated. When your partner is angry, it is most important to not confront the emotion, to not oppose anger with anger. If the anger does not have a legitimate base, it will not last long. It will dissipate as the energy behind it is consumed. When it dissipates, you can then deal with the issues. If it does have a legitimate basis, agree with the emotion. Say something like, "I know you have a good reason to be angry," and really mean it. This is not a diplomatic game. You cannot hide behind an untrue feeling.

In agreeing with the anger, you expedite the anger process, and help the emotion go through the stages it must go through. If you use anger to counter anger, it will only perpetuate the emotion: it will persist, and even take root. If you allow it to flow, it will go. Give it time and space, and allow it to pass through. Do not hold on to it or obstruct it; do not try to force it to speed up.

Guide it without forcing it. This is the best way to resolve the problem and return to an untroubled state.

It is important to realize that the soul is ultimately pure. As a Zen koan says, "The body is a wisdom-tree; the mind is a mirror." The original nature is always clear and shining. Negative energies are things that pass through us; they are not part of us.

We are what we think. Ten thousand dharmas manifest from thought; ten thousand troubles also manifest from thought.

Thought processes create and perpetuate suffering. Take stress, for example. It is a product of fast-paced modern life. But when stress becomes a focus for public concern, we add fuel to it and give it legitimacy. Stress management programs give stress power and make it seem normal. A small problem can become bigger if it is fed by "treatment." For example, we now need to "attack" stress to deal with it, which causes more stress. This approach is often self-defeating.

Like other emotional entanglements, it is best to not attack or counter the emotion directly, but to become aware of it, and see it clearly. When we can see its components, and how it arises out of circumstances, we realize that it has no solid foundation. As we come to see the disturbing emotion, it will come to dissipate.

To create good relationships, resonate with positive feelings from your partner. Focus on the positive; allow negative feelings to pass through and away. If things don't resolve, examine yourself before you try to analyze your partner.

Remember, in Yin-Yang Theory, Yin and Yang go together. If we recognize that the problem is Yin and the solution is Yang, we can see that when there is a problem, there is a solution. A natural solution is always easy and readily available.

Give each other room and space. Never hold grudges as weapons for future revenge: you only consume and taint your own energy.

In ancient times, most marriages were arranged by the family. But these marriages often worked out much better than modern partnerships. Is the problem with society? With the other partner? Or with oneself?

Diamonds Are Not Forever: Qi Is

Body and emotions are both manifestations of qi. Dealing with things at the level of body and emotions is more limited than dealing with things at the level of qi. To deal with things from a higher level, one has to be able to enter a simpler state of being, one in which harmony and balance already exist, and guide the levels "below" to enter into harmony themselves. When qi is abundant, things below happen naturally and effectively. For example, when one has an abundance of energy, one is less likely to be tired or frustrated, and one can deal spontaneously and effectively with difficulties as they arise. When one has less energy, small difficulties can be hard to resolve, and can amplify a general state of disorganization. Although there are specific techniques for managing mood and behavior, they come to seem unnecessarily complicated if one can simply increase one's energy level, perhaps just by getting more rest. From this point of view, the more specific techniques are like remedies for temporary imbalances, but they are not fundamental solutions.

Many people, when dealing with emotional problems, experiment with meditation or similar approaches as a way to get answers. This is a very good thing to do, but people often get discouraged even before they give meditation a try because it can seem like a long and complicated process. But it doesn't have to be.

Actually, meditation is directly related to qi. Mind and qi are closely related. In the same way that qi manifests as physical processes and events, mind, especially intention, manifests as events on the level of qi. There are many exercises that are directly related to qi, like Tai Chi Chuan (the Tai Chi exercise), various Qi Gong systems, and some kinds of meditation. These can be very rewarding if studied with a qualified teacher, but they are hard to learn from a book. There is, however, a simple method of meditation, which can be learned easily, that helps to develop balanced manifestations of qi.

The Fifteen-Minute Meditation

There is a very common experience that people share when they first begin to meditate: when trying to stabilize and calm the mind, it seems to become even busier. On the other hand, when trying to to avoid controlling the mind, it will continue to wander. Paying attention to a basic breathing pattern can shorten or eliminate this mind wandering. There are many suggestions about how to do this, but the following is one of the most effective.

Begin by sitting comfortably, either on a chair or cross-legged on the floor. Allow your body to become naturally erect, with the crown of your head pointed upward, and your neck naturally straight. Put your hands, one over the other, in front of, or covering, your belly, or just put them on your legs, whichever makes you feel most comfortable.

Pay attention to breathing out. Don't think about inhaling: just be aware of exhaling. You will soon find yourself becoming calmer and more relaxed; your breathing will become slower and quieter.

Then, as you continue to be aware of the process of exhaling, let your awareness deepen. While exhaling, let your awareness sink downward, as if it is sinking into your abdomen.

As you continue, you will feel your exhalation getting deeper, and your awareness sinking more deeply with it, until you feel you are exhaling not only from your chest and abdomen, but also from your legs, and down into the ground. Your breathing will become even slower and quieter. Finally, you will feel that you are exhaling not only through your belly and legs, but through your arms and your whole body. Your body will begin to feel an expansion and contraction with each exhalation and inhalation. As your awareness follows this sense of expansion and contraction, your mind will naturally come to stability and stop wandering. You will experience a surge of energy that fills and warms your body; this is the beginning of the meditative state.

This is one of the most effective ways to enter a meditative state. A fifteen-minute session is better, but even if you can only get a five- or ten-minute break, you can practice this method. You will be able to connect with your inner self and with the universe, and be nourished by the abundant qi of the universe. This state of tranquility is the foundation for any practice that reaches toward a higher state of wisdom.

This exercise is very simple. It is not a challenge. This connection with the energy of the universe can provide what you need to support a healthy body, balanced emotions, and a sound mind. With regular practice, you will discover that you are well, that everyone around you is lovely, and that your relationship with your partner has become refreshed.

Body, mind, and qi are three closely related aspects of human existence. In any human activity, within ourselves or in relationships, they are crucial factors. A healthy body, a peaceful mind, and an abundance of qi lead to a balanced foundation for any romantic interaction.

7

Food and Love

Of the three most basic human needs—food, clothing, and shelter—food may be the most important. People turn to food for many things: basic survival, health, and strength, and even compensation for various problems of life. As soon as we get beyond the minimum needed for bare survival, the kind of food we eat varies immensely, reflecting the vast variety of human characteristics, in culture, environment, and religion.

Whenever we talk about love and romance, about the relationships between Yin and Yang energies, we always have to get back to the fundamental concepts of a healthy body and a balanced mind. Food plays a major role in our health and our emotions. In dealing with romance, we cannot ignore the power of food.

There are people who say, "You are what you eat." It is true that the kind and quality of food that people eat shape their lives; it is also true, however, that the kind and quality of food readily available to people are shaped by their communities, and reflect different approaches to life. What we eat, and how we prepare our food, has a close relationship to our other activities and other aspects of our lives. Our food not only affects our health and emotions, it reflects our values and taste.

Different cultures and regions have developed wide varieties of foods, and these foods have changed and developed with time. Food is a big part of every culture, and it also plays a major part in the enjoyment of life.

Food Is Not Just Chemicals

People say that healthy food makes for a healthy body and mind—but what, really, is healthy food? What makes a diet truly healthy and balanced?

Before we can answer these questions, we have to reexamine the ideas of modern nutritional science about what food is made of. Modern nutritional science tends to classify foods into five categories: carbohydrates, proteins, fats, vitamins, and minerals. All are crucial for good health. An adequate diet, consisting of balanced proportions of these nutrients, is supposed to be sufficient for good health. But people are not like cars, able to run on anything that is put through a tube as long as it is chemically correct. Are foods just the chemical nutrients into which they can be analyzed? Or is there something more—something we can see if we look at the subject from a different point of view? And, even more, is there a universal standard for deciding what kind of food is healthy, and what kind of diet is balanced?

There are a vast number of variables that affect the relationship between food and health, among them age, region, seasons, profession or job, and the source of the food. It seems, then, that it is not possible to set a universal standard, one that will work for everyone in every situation. Nor is it scientifically valid to do so. Some people rarely consume vegetables and fruit, but live on meat and dairy products; others almost never eat meat or other animal products, and live only on vegetables.

Modern nutritionists emphasize the importance of eating an abundance of fruit and vegetables, and see them as a necessary part of a good diet. However, there are places in the world where vegetables are simply not available—is the diet of people who live in such places unbalanced? People do well when they eat the food of their region. For example, years ago people in Mongolia hardly ever ate vegetables because they were not readily available, but they used yogurt and tea to supplement their meat diet. As long as the tastes of the food they ate were balanced, and derived from their own region, they were able to maintain their health and strength.

What, then, can we use to guide us in selecting the right kinds of food to promote health and romance? The first thing is to follow what is traditional for the culture and region in which we find ourselves. The traditional local diets give us guidelines for the kinds of food that have worked for the people who live in a particular place, and have followed a particular way of life for a long time.

The traditional Chinese way of looking at food developed in a special way because of the vast and varied territory of China and the highly diverse ways of life followed by the different people who live in its different regions. Each area, each mode of life, developed foods that were suitable to it—but the general Chinese medical and scientific tradition then looked at these differences and tried to account for them in terms of traditional approaches to understanding nature.

The traditional Chinese approach to food focuses on more than just nutrients: it focuses on color, texture, taste, and smell. These qualities are seen as energetic qualities. Each of these qualities conveys a special kind of energy or qi. Food is ultimately a form of energy, one that manifests in many ways. This energy can be analyzed from the point of view of chemical (and caloric) composition, color, physical form, taste, and smell, as shown in figure 7.1.

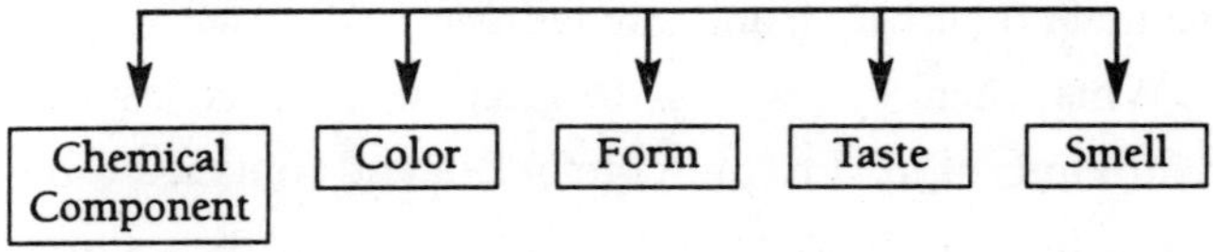

Figure 7.1: Food energy

For example, take different kinds of celery. One kind of celery is small, but has a strong scent. Another kind of celery is much bigger, and also much blander. The bigger kind may have more volume, and perhaps even more calories, than the smaller kind—but the smaller kind has a more intense energetic effect.

Foods and herbs also carry a particular kind of memory, related to how that particular herb sample has been processed or prepared. Take, for example, the herb ginseng. If you slice the root, grind it, and use the powder to make a hot drink, it will have one effect; if you boil the whole root and drink the broth, it will have another. The different *forms* from which the drink is prepared have different effects because the forms carry the energy of the material from which they were prepared, as well as the energy of the original material. This is what happens with homeopathic medicines, which are so diluted that, even theoretically, no molecule of the original chemical is present. Yet the medicine is still effective because the energy and information are still present in the solution.

Some newer methods of food cultivation that depend on modern chemical technology focus on increasing the size and amount of food, and shortening the production cycle, but do not take into account the energetic (qi) factors. The result is that there may be more food in terms of mere quantity, but no increase in the total energy provided. People who live on such foods may seem to be well nourished, but still lack energy. This is because there is an imbalance between their intake of chemical nutrients (in caloric and nutritional terms) and energetic nutrients (in qi terms).

Tastes and the Five Elements

In traditional China, foods were classified in terms of Yin and Yang, in terms of the five elements, and in terms of the particular energy meridians of the human body that they would enter and affect. With that approach, a balanced diet is one with balanced energies.

Color and taste also have interrelationships: each affects the others, and each affects particular organs. These relationships can be understood using Five Element Theory model, as shown in table 7.2.

Element	Taste	Color	Organs
Wood	Sour	Green	Liver & Gall Bladder
Fire	Bitter	Red	Heart & Small Intestine
Earth	Sweet	Yellow	Spleen & Stomach
Metal	Spicy	White	Lungs & Large Intestine
Water	Salty	Black	Kidneys & Bladder

Table 7.2: The Five Elements and food table

As we can see from the table, each of the five elements is related to one of the five tastes: sour, bitter, sweet, spicy (hot), and salty. A balanced diet is based on the balance of tastes. Sweet (earth) is the central flavor, as earth is the central element, and thus sweetness is the dominant or neutral factor in all foods. The key is to adjust the other tastes (salty, bitter, spicy, and sour) around the central sweet taste.

Balance of the five tastes often comes from natural desire. After vigorous exercise, athletes, or other people who do a lot of hard labor, often prefer their food a bit salty. Pregnant women frequently yearn for sour foods, without knowing explicitly that sour, being a flavor and linked with the wood element, assists the building and growth processes of pregnancy. In cold weather, spicy or hot foods taste especially good.

These preferences are natural bodily responses. People doing hard labor may not know that they need to replace the salt lost in sweat, and pregnant women may not necessarily know that they are yearning for sour food because of its importance for the growth process. They don't have to: their bodies provide the impulse. The natural yearning for balancing tastes does not require training; it has direct connections with physiological needs.

Thousands of years ago, Chinese medical theory also established the relationships between the five tastes and various internal organs. For example, sour is connected with the liver and gall bladder; bitter is connected with the heart and small intestine; sweet is related to the stomach and spleen; spiciness is related to the lungs and large intestine; saltiness is related to the kidneys and bladder.

In China, food is always regarded as one form of medicine. The first step in adjusting physiological imbalances, and even psychological imbalances, is to adjust the diet. To do this, one has to know how the tastes interact with physiological and psychological functions—something that Five Element Theory helps us to understand.

Have you ever bitten your tongue while eating? This doesn't happen because you are too nervous or eating too quickly, but because you have an overactive heart function. If you supply some additional bitterness by eating some raw turnip, or some stir-fried bitter melon, you can adjust this irregularity of the heart function (because bitterness is connected with the heart).

Five Element Theory also suggests that eating food that is too salty will increase the burden on the kidneys, and may damage them (because saltiness is related to the kidneys). Similarly, people with liver problems should avoid food that is too spicy; people with heart problems should avoid salt; people with spleen problems should avoid sourness; people with lung problems should avoid bitterness; people with kidney problems should avoid excessive sweetness. This is because each element has an element that it controls, and also has an element that controls it, as shown in figure 7.3 on the following page.

It is hard to quantify the balance of tastes. But once you are aware that these relationships can exist, you can

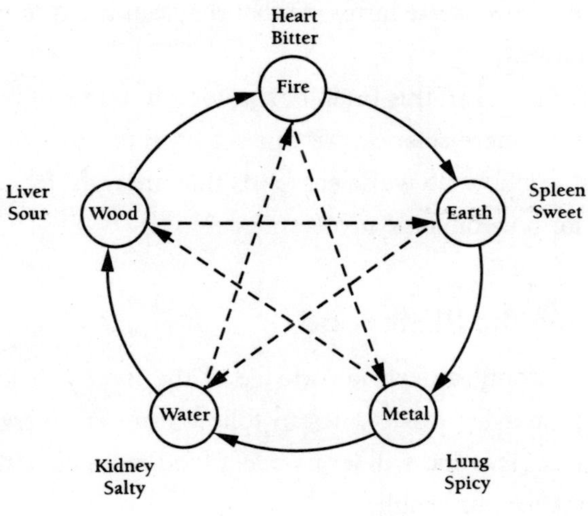

Figure 7.3: Relationships between the five elements, organs, and taste

begin to learn from your own experience how they exist in your own life and in the lives of people you know.

Color, smell, and form also have their links with the five elements. Each set of qualities interacts with the others, in the same way that the basic tastes do. All these factors have their internal relationships as well.

It is important to remember that the classification of tastes, colors, smells, and forms in terms of the five elemental categories is, fundamentally, a classification in terms of five kinds of energy and the relationships between those kinds of energies. The model of the elements makes it possible for people to grasp an abstract process in concrete terms, so that they can use it in their daily lives.

Having taken this brief look at food in terms of traditional Chinese science, we can get back to our original question: how do we select foods that are right for us—and for our romantic involvements?

Picking the Right Food

Even without a deep knowledge of the theory of food, there are a few basic rules to follow from an energetic point of view that will let us select food more effectively to enhance our health.

First, eat as much locally grown food as possible. Any food that is traditional and local has been used for a reason. The effects of the region have influenced the choice of foods, and it is wise to take this into account. Food growing in a certain place resonates with the energy of that place, and with the energy of the people who live there. So if you live in a place where fruit grows abundantly, eat fruit; if you live in a place where barley grows, eat barley.

Second, eat seasonal food. Food grows at a certain time for a reason. Watermelon grows in the summer because it dissipates heat. Foods that are harvested in the fall provide the extra energy needed to get through the winter. In the modern world, with fast transportation to shorten distances, what we eat often comes from thousands of miles away, where even the seasons are different. Modern storage technology lets us have almost any food in any season. This convenience unfortunately enables us to forget the energies of time and space that shape us.

Third, eat as much variety as possible. The modern emphasis on efficiency and productivity has led to the dominance of mass farming. Supermarkets seem to be filled, but they have the same foods everywhere. Local varieties are lost. If you have even a little space in a yard, plant a small garden, and grow things that are hard to find in the supermarket.

Fourth, eat as much fresh food as possible. Freshness is not only a matter of taste and nutritional value, it is also a matter of energetic value. The energetic value of food decreases in proportion to the length of time it is stored. Fresh-picked corn has a very different, and much sweeter, flavor than corn that has been processed and stored. The flavor of frozen fruit is far from the flavor of fresh-picked fruit. Anyone who has ever eaten ripe, fresh-picked grapefruit knows the difference between it and the kind of grapefruit usually available in a supermarket.

If you follow these rules, you are more likely to find that you are eating a healthy diet. Naturally, the healthier you are, the more you can enjoy your romantic relationships.

Eating Well

In addition to choosing foods well, it is just as important to eat them well. A few simple guidelines can help us to understand what this means.

First, listen to your stomach and to your body—before you listen to the experts—when choosing what to eat. Our bodies constantly tell us what we need. When we feel cold, our bodies are telling us to dress more warmly; when we feel thirsty, our bodies are telling us we need to drink more water. When we are tired and need to rest, our eyelids will close. Similarly, our stomachs will tell us when to eat, how much to eat, and when to stop eating. When you find yourself yearning for a particular kind of food or flavor, you probably have a real need for it. Yet we tend to disregard this kind of information, and listen to information from outside, to the point that some *people weigh their food by the gram.*

Second, really enjoy your food. Take your time, and eat mindfully. There is more to eating than just refueling. If you eat too fast, by the time you feel full, you have already eaten too much—and eating too much kills romantic feelings. (People who eat in a hurry probably make love in a hurry, too!) How we eat, and our emotional state while eating, have a direct effect on how the food is digested and used. Nowadays, people live at such a fast pace that they treat food as merely a source of calories. People even eat when driving. A drive-through restaurant is like a feeding machine, a gas station for people.

Third, don't eat when you are angry, stressed, or otherwise energetically unbalanced. Your body might still be able to process the chemicals, but not the energy of the food.

Fourth, try to eat as much home cooking as possible. The process of preparing the food makes a difference in the energy of the food. A home-cooked meal is made with, and transmits, a very different kind of energy than commercially prepared food. A sweater knitted by your mother feels more comfortable than one you buy in the store; the same thing is true with food. People often say that grandma's chicken soup is the best medicine for a cold. It's not just the soup: it's the tender loving care with which it is made that adds a special energy to the soup.

Fifth, eat when you are hungry and drink when you are thirsty, but never eat until you are full. We are too dominated by habits and customs that make us eat set meals at set times, whether we need them (or want them) or not. The extra food just takes more energy to digest. This is why, when your stomach is too full, you become sleepy. All your energy is going into digestion. It is better to eat less more frequently than to eat a lot at one meal. When you are too hungry, you can damage your qi; when you are too full, you can impair your breathing: shortness of breath is common after eating a large meal. Never go to sleep with a full stomach; this can lead to excess mucus, which can make breathing difficult.

Sixth, always maintain a balance. Do not eat too much of any one thing, no matter how good it may be. Excess can turn a good thing into a bad thing.

While it is important to enjoy food, it is important to remember that the basic purpose of food is to provide health and strength. Enjoyment, important as it is, is an added bonus.

Avoid the First Mistake

Mistakes usually come in pairs. When you make one mistake, you will often make another, though it may not be clear that the second one comes from the first.

When people drift away from traditional good eating patterns, they develop various disorders. To counteract these, various remedies appear, and these remedies are often the source of new problems. But if the first mistake hadn't been made, there would have been no need for the remedies, and no danger of abusing them. Instead of trying harder and harder to find the right combination of remedies, we should try to get back to eating the right kinds of food from the right place at the right time.

For example, if you find you have been eating too much, you may decide to go on a diet. But dieting itself can cause problems, and can even lead to the cycle of binging and purging, which we now recognize as bulimia, an eating disorder.

Diet Programs Are Not the Road to Romance

The consequences of not following the natural way include problems such as eating disorders, obesity, and many other things. In developed countries, like the United States, people become obsessed with trying to get their bodies back into the "right" shape. Indeed, obesity contributes to over half of modern health problems. And this leads to the constant invention of new diet programs, which often completely contradict each other. One expert tells everyone to eat a high protein diet; another will recommend a carbohydrate diet; both will sell thousands of books, and may even help a few people. But it is not possible to simply pick a popular expert and expect to get a guaranteed benefit from following that expert's program.

People become overweight for different reasons; no one program provides a universal solution, nor can it. Instead of indulging in diet programs, a person who is overweight should try to understand the cause of his or her problem.

Why do people become overweight? From eating too much and exercising too little. Why do people overeat? Why don't people exercise regularly? People might overeat for emotional reasons, as a way of managing anxiety. People who are depressed may eat more, using food to fill up a sense of emptiness. Not only can anxiety cause unbalanced eating, unbalanced eating can also cause anxiety and other forms of distress. And the more overweight a person is, the less energy he or she has, which makes exercise all the more difficult.

People in traditional societies may have also experienced distress, but they weren't subject to the pressures of modern life that distort so many other aspects of our natural rhythms and patterns. The root cause of much of our modern problem with overeating and lack of exercise is our general situation, characterized by massive disruption of these natural rhythms and patterns.

Are Nutritional Supplements the Answer?

Nowadays, as material goods become more and more abundant, nutritional supplements have emerged as a hot new product. There are over fifteen thousand nutritional supplements currently on the market, supposedly in response to nutritional deficiencies or the need to boost energy. Ironically, this has come about at a time when the food supply seems more abundant than ever before.

Do we really need these supplements? If we say "yes," then we open up a huge can of worms. Which supplements really work? What kinds do we need? What are the ideal quantities of each? What about possible side effects, or conflicts between different supplements? What is the ideal combination for a specific person's needs?

Every manufacturer will claim that its products are not only effective but also necessary, but no one can tell you for sure whether or not you need a particular product. A great deal depends on the individual: health conditions, lifestyle, age, and so on.

The natural way is the simple way. As long as you stay with a balanced diet, and follow the simple rules we have suggested, you will not need to be too concerned about nutritional supplements. Do not make your life more complicated than it needs to be. Chances are, it is already complicated enough.

When there is a problem, seek the fundamental solution by seeking the source of the problem. Don't look for remedies that will only create secondary problems while attempting to fix the original one.

Candlelight Cooking

People in all cultures throughout history have been interested in the potential of food to increase sexual energy. Aphrodisiac foods, from common to exotic, exist in many cultures and traditions.

It is true that some foods are more likely to enhance romantic moods and promote sexual energy. Commonly known aphrodisiac foods include such seafood as shrimp, lobster, oysters, clams, sea cucumber, caviar, and shark fins. There are also land-based foods, such as venison, lamb, and eggs of all sorts; vegetables such as Chinese chives, celery, basil, garlic, coriander, green onions, and ginger; nuts like cashews and walnuts; and fruits like dates, figs, and mangos. Honey is also effective, as are spices like anise and bay leaves. All of these are commonly available. There are also more medicinal vegetables, such as ginseng, lotus seed, lyceum berries, and so on. In traditional Chinese medicine, there is an abundance of information available about aphrodisiac foods, but we are keeping things simple by looking mainly at foods that are commonly available in the market.

Ingredients are important, but preparation can make all the difference. Chinese cooking classifies the preparation process in terms of Yin and Yang. Deep frying, roasting, and baking are regarded as Yang processes; steaming, stewing, and slow cooking are Yin processes. To maximize the effects of ingredients, it is best to prepare them using Yin processes. Deep-frying and other Yang processes should be used with restraint. Deep-fried shrimp is less potent than shrimp sautéed in wine.

Food combinations are also important. The right combinations can produce synergistic enhancements of mood and energy. Cashews stir-fried with unshelled shrimp, oysters eaten raw, Chinese chives cooked with scrambled eggs, lamb stew, green onion with beef (maybe with oyster sauce), celery with lean pork, basil and lean pork simmered in wine, lobster stir-fried with ginger, chicken stewed with ginseng—these are examples of the kinds of foods people can easily make at home.

Chocolate is regarded as a very romantic food. Cheese is also surprisingly effective. Cheese-eating people generally have more sexual energy than those who don't eat cheese, all other things being equal.

An infusion of lyceum berries in sherry or whisky can be very effective—but the berries can also be put into soup, like chicken or duck soup, with good effects. Traditionally, it was said that men who were going to be away from home for a long period of time should avoid eating lyceum berries to avoid inappropriate sexual desire.

Interesting as these recipes can be, one should not give them too much importance. As long as you have a balanced diet and good health, you might not need any of the extra mileage provided by such dishes. The best source of sexual energy is a healthy body.

Romantic Dining

The romance of dining has much more to do with the atmosphere than with the food itself. The food is just a vehicle to convey the atmosphere. This is why the setting is at least as important as the food. In romantic dining, it is better to eat less than it is to eat more. Food should be a medium for exchange of energy, rather than the focus of the energy.

Don't serve big steaks, huge lobsters, or other fancy foods to impress your partner. If people eat too much, it will be too easy for them to forget all about romance—and fall asleep. A high-fat meal also tends to reduce sexual desire.

It is important to have a setting in which there is a dynamic balance of Yin and Yang to create a rhythm. This is why it is good to move from one setting or environment to another, to provide a mixture of settings. For example, one might eat dinner in one place and have dessert or drinks in another. This can provide a good mix of formal and casual, and public and private. This shifts attention from the food to the relationship that extends throughout the changing phases and settings of the meal, and opens up a sense of extension and expansion.

When people are not well acquainted, an environment that is somewhat more Yang may be better at the beginning; as the relationship deepens, a more Yin environment may be appropriate. Yang features include round tables, brighter lights and colors, and more open space; Yin features include square tables, darker lights and colors, and more enclosed space.

Final Thoughts About Food

Food affects our health and moods. But there is much more to it. Since we spend a lot of time securing, preparing, and enjoying food, food can be a great medium for establishing or enhancing a romantic relationship. This is why, when we think about food and romance, it is important to encompass the whole process of dealing with food.

Any part of the act of obtaining, preparing, and eating food, when conducted together, can enhance the relationship. Sharing these activities unobtrusively enhances the relationship itself. This is why it is often better to cook in than to dine out. Sharing the process, and not just the product, brings the relationship into every aspect of life

8

Desire and Unity

The attraction between Yin and Yang energies is the fundamental law of nature. As we have defined them, Yin and Yang must coexist, and cannot exist in isolation. This is true on every scale: in the cosmos, in the solar system, on the planet, and in the relationship between men and women. All of these are manifestations of the same interchange.

Every living thing has three components: matter, energy, and information. "Matter" refers to physical manifestations of all sorts. "Energy" refers to the forces that carry out all the transforming functions of living things. "Information" has to do with soul and spirit, understanding and memory. In a human organism, the matter level has to do with flesh and bones; the energy level has to do with metabolic processes; the information level has to do with thoughts, memories, spiritual realizations, and will. The ultimate attraction and unification of living things involves the unification of all three of these components. That is, there are connections on the three levels of information, energy, and matter. The physical (material) connection plays a necessary and important role in the ultimate unification.

Sexuality demonstrates the highest manifestation of physical unification. The eternal cycle of life depends on this vehicle to continue. Beyond pleasure, and beyond physical and emotional fulfillment, it carries a sacred mission: to allow a species to continue to exist. For most animals, sexuality seems to have much more to do with reproduction than it has to do with pleasure. For humans, however, especially with modern birth control, sexuality is often simply a source of pleasure. Throughout human history, in fact, this tendency has always existed. Some psychologists even suggest that the ultimate goal underlying all human striving is sex. Whether this is true or not, it does point to the importance that sexual desire has had in human history.

Sexual union is the natural result of mutual attraction. Sexual union transforms a relationship. When sex is added to any relationship, it indicates a new level of intensity and of mutual revelation and trust.

Do You Feel Anything Yet?

In modern times, with the so-called sexual revolution, the perception of sex as primarily a source of pleasure has undermined the sacredness of sex, leading to a downturn in the quality of sexual experience.

With increasing industrialization, human life and human activities have become more mechanized. It is almost as though people have come to work for machines, on the machines' terms. Subtlety of feeling, sensitivity, and the inner side of life have become lost. People tend to respond in a simple on-and-off fashion, without much sense of gradation. Furthermore, it seems that people need increasingly stronger stimuli to have any effect: subtle stimuli seem to have no effect at all. Music is louder, colors stronger, cars faster, and architecture more intrusive and outrageous, all in an attempt to get our attention.

But the stronger the stimulation, the more sensitivity diminishes, requiring even stronger stimuli. A vicious cycle is set up, until people find themselves going to extremes to obtain an effect that, a few generations ago, could be achieved very simply.

Industrialization seems to be a great success, because it has led to an abundance of things that once were scarce. This is the Yang aspect of the process. But Yang is always accompanied by Yin, and the Yin aspect of the process is that we have come to lose touch with the more subtle aspects of life, and the senses of intuition and sensitivity that are necessary to perceive them. We have lost touch with the subtle inner side of nature and life.

For example, because of the advances of horticulture, and the pressures of competitive marketing, people notice only the biggest, brightest, and most extravagant flowers. They have lost the ability to appreciate the old, simple flowers, like the beauty of the small dandelion. Our senses are so bombarded with stimulation that they have become fatigued, and unable to respond. Many of us cannot enjoy simple things, and things that are naturally available: gentle breezes rippling the water, the moon rising between the mountains, or new buds unfolding on the trees in spring.

It is no surprise that the physical side of sexual relationships has also taken a downturn. Sadly, it seems that relationships have to be strong, active, and vibrant, even violent, just to give people a sense that they are really having an effect on each other. We can no longer understand old poetry in which a glance between lovers can be fulfilling, or the touch of a hand can be like an electrical shock. In old movies, the actor and actress kiss at the end; in modern movies they jump into bed at the beginning.

Books, laboratory investigations, and a focus on technique dominate the teaching of sexuality. This is a big change from traditional approaches. It is seldom mentioned that intimacy can and should be achieved before physical contact. Two people can make love without touching, just in getting to know each other as human beings. This can be a very natural and beautiful process, but the couple must take time, and refrain from the tendency to become physically intimate before the emotional attunement takes place. If they let the desire for intimacy grow and focus as they find each other becoming more and more compatible and loving, they will feel their energies merging and interacting. This is really the foundation process for developing a memorable sexual relationship.

Sex is the ultimate symbol of the unification of Yin and Yang in human experience. In Taoist tradition, sex is regarded as being a gateway to either heaven or hell. With proper guidance, sex can enhance health, balance emotions, and lead to higher states of being, even the kind of experience of egoless unification that people learn to achieve after practicing meditation for a long time. But, at the same time, the improper use of or indulgence in sex can also lead to poor health and spiritual collapse. It is because of this potential for abuse that, in many cultures, sexuality is regarded as the seed of evil, and sexual promiscuity or indulgence is regarded as the greatest form of corruption.

Right Time and Right Space

Sex should be approached holistically, with due regard for the factors of time and space. Like other organic wholes, human bodies are open systems. During sexual activity, the merging of the Yin and Yang aspects of the human entity into a greater unity makes it far more open than usual. External influences become far more significant. This is why external events and conditions can have an especially strong impact during sexual activity. For this reason, traditional teaching recommends avoiding extremes during sex. This means that sex should be avoided during extremely hot or extremely cold weather, or extreme natural conditions. Extreme weather involves an imbalance of qi flow, and will induce a similar effect in the human body. Similarly, people should also avoid making love when they are in extreme emotional or physical states.

For most people, for practical reasons, sexual activity takes place in the evening. In traditional teachings, it is said that, in general, male sexual energy is more abundant in the evening than it is in the morning, and sexual activity at night will tend to be more nourishing for women because of this. In the same way, in early morning female energy is more abundant, so sex in the early morning will tend to be more beneficial for males. These are not rigid rules, but useful guidelines for assessing one's experiences. Each couple should assess the ways in which these patterns manifest in their relationship.

Timing is often governed largely by passion and opportunity—but the points mentioned previously should be taken into account as much as possible.

In terms of space, people get the most out of sex when they are in a balanced and peaceful situation. Naturally, a private, secure, and protected place is best. A cozy bedroom with good Feng Shui (as discussed in chapter 3) will be an ideal place. There are people who pursue adventure, and look for the most exotic places and times for the sake of added excitement. In the long term, however, they will have to endure the negative consequences of this pattern of activity. There is nothing wrong with creativity, with going outside or beyond routine. But there is plenty of space for creativity within the basic traditional guidelines. Moving from one kind of balanced and peaceful place to another can add variety and encourage creativity without exposing us to the dangers that come from extremes of imbalance or risk.

The Ultimate Technique

Fulfillment always comes from inside, not from outside. It is true that many books focus on sexual technique, and a focus on technique does have a certain value. But there is no technique or position or device that can replace the most important factor, which is love. *Love is the ultimate technique.* If mutual feeling and attraction are there, the unification of these energies will elevate feelings no matter how little you do. A simple hug or kiss, or just holding hands, can give a sense of great abundance. Without a strong sense of love, merely physical stimulation can leave you feeling tired or empty—an anticlimax after the climax.

In lovemaking, it is important to be sensitive to each other's rhythms and processes. It is good when lovers can reach climax at the same time. This requires patience, awareness, mutual nourishment, and sensitivity. For men, the time-structure of sex is obvious. For women, the sexual cycle is subtler, and the signs of sexual arousal are also more individual and subtle. Remember: men, in general, need space; women need time. Only with love and care on the male side, and open communication on the female side, can the two cycles be integrated. A great deal can be said about the physiology of the sexual cycle—but when love is absent, it is unlikely that people will be motivated to take the physiology of the cycle into account. In a relationship in which only one partner is receiving fulfillment, the other partner will sooner or later become disengaged. Yin-Yang Theory states that if the relationship is lopsided, the Tai Chi (the world) of the relationship will contract and become more limited. Only when there is balance does a Tai Chi system continue to flourish.

It's a matter of love, not lovemaking. Physical stimulation itself only lasts for a relatively short time (no matter how much one works to prolong it). Certain physical accessories, however, can be helpful. Anything that can create a proper atmosphere, like candles, incense, fresh flowers, or scented oils, can enhance and support feelings that are already there, and make them easier to express and share. A gentle, thorough massage with sesame oil, well-known to detoxify and increase heat, can be a valuable kind of foreplay. With abundant love as the base, gentleness, sensitivity, and responsiveness to each other's feelings will nourish a relationship that will last a long time.

Climax Is Only Half Way

Yin and Yang energies exhibit different characters. Yang is manifesting, outward, aggressive, dynamic, expansive. Yin is inward, subtle, responsive, and withdrawing. To Yang energy, the highest manifestation is reaching the goal; to Yin energy, completion means returning from the goal to the point of origin. Climax is like reaching the top of a mountain. For Yang energy, that's the goal, and the rest is irrelevant. From the Yin point of view, the journey is not complete until one has come back from the mountaintop.

Often men think only of manifestation, and do not realize or appreciate the importance of the second half of the journey. To women, however, the second half of the journey is as important as the first. It is essential for them to go through the entire process. Men should realize the importance of completing the cycle.

Yin-Yang Theory also provides another guideline. When genital stimulation is too intense, leading to a tendency to hasten ejaculation, it is good to balance the excess energy in the genitals with attention at the other end of the body, at the crown of the head. Focusing one's attention there can help redistribute and balance the energy throughout the body, help make intercourse last longer, and make for a more balanced and harmonious energy exchange.

Yang is naturally dynamically expansive: to be well balanced, it needs to have an element of restraint or control (Yin). Yin, on the other hand, being naturally reserved and contained, needs a quality of unblocked openness (Yang) to be well balanced. In other words, men, as carriers of expansive energy, should exercise control over their expansive energy. Women, as carriers of contained energy, should allow themselves to let go In lovemaking, men should control themselves, and women should allow themselves to be completely free and unrestrained. When men are controlled, they can more easily delay their climax; when women are unrestrained, they find it easier to reach their climax. In this way, being better balanced within themselves, the male and female energies can achieve a more balanced climax together.

In a symphony, the music leads us along a journey, lifting us up, then bringing us back at the end. This pattern is a good model for a sexual encounter. The symphony doesn't stop at the third movement—nor should a sexual encounter.

Sex and Health

Sex has a crucial role in carrying on life and relationships. However, many people do not realize that it also plays an important role in health.

Well-balanced sex can enhance health; unbalanced sex can have a negative effect on health. In the long tradition of Taoist teaching, there is a great amount of knowledge about sex. Taoism in fact may contain the oldest and most influential tradition of sex education. As we have said earlier, every human endeavor has three aspects: time, space, and people. The same thing is true for sex: the right time, the right place, and the right partner are all important.

There are some basic principles that people can use to safeguard their health in the context of sexual relations.

1. External factors and events are important. This refers to the human sexual cycles and to the patterns of nature. Sexual union is a moment of openness and vulnerability, when people are permeable to outside influences. It is important to avoid having sex when the heavens are in tumult or imbalance: during storms, in extremes of heat or cold, or during intense, changing weather patterns. Ironically, in big storms, when the electricity goes out, people jump into bed—but this may not be the best time to do so. Similarly, tradition recommends avoiding

sex during the full or new moons, or at the equinoxes or solstices, because these are extreme conditions.

2. Intercourse should occur when you are in the right physical and emotional state. Never have sex when you are too tired, too drunk, too hungry, or too full—nor when depressed, angry, or emotionally unstable. When you have sex during such times, you tend to lose energy rather than to benefit from union with your complementary energy. Unfortunately, people often use sex as an escape from depression, thus eventually maintaining or intensifying their depression. Women should be cautious about having sex during pregnancy, since intense physical reactions might, in some circumstances, harm the fetus.

3. Avoid both overindulgence and prolonged abstinence. Overindulging tends to deplete energy, and speed up the aging process. (Overindulgence is often an attempt to compensate for something one lacks: this is why it can lead to intensified feelings of depression and emptiness.) Too much abstinence without proper guidance of the energy can lead to frustration, bad temper, and intense compensatory indulgence in other things, like eating or gambling.

4. Follow the pattern and rhythm of nature. Winter is colder than summer; young people are more active than old people. The same thing applies to sexual activity. Energy begins to manifest in spring, and peaks in summer; in fall it tends to return downward. Thus

sex is better to have more frequently in spring and summer than in fall or winter. You might have sex more frequently when you are younger, but it can be a mistake to try to keep up the same frequency when you are older.

Eight Nourishments and Seven Damages

Traditional teaching provides many specific guidelines for sexual activity. One classical Taoist system involves what are called the "Eight Nourishments and Seven Damages," which are concrete methods for nourishing sexual energies in daily life, as well as before, during, and after sexual activity.

The Eight Nourishments deal with three phases of sexual activity: what to do in daily life, what to do during intercourse, and what to do after intercourse to help balance energies.

1. Nourish qi daily. In the morning, after waking up, sit and meditate. Stretch your spine while you sit, relax your hips, lift or contract your perineum, and visualize the focus of energy around your genitals. If you make this part of your routine for at least twenty minutes every day, you will never lack sexual energy.

2. Swallow the qi. During meditation, you will find an abundance of saliva collecting. Swallow it, visualizing the saliva descending to the region of your genitals.

3. Pay attention to timing. Before intercourse, prolong foreplay until both partners are experiencing height-

ened sexual desire. Only then should you go on to intercourse.

4. During intercourse, relax your spine, contract or lift your perineum, and guide your qi downward.

5. During intercourse, avoid excessively fast movements and sudden or agitated motions. The slower one's motions, the more the Yin and Yang energy will interact and coalesce.

6. Men should engage in sexual activity only when erect, and should not continue activity when not charged with energy, which is called holding or accumulating qi.

7. Toward the end of intercourse, take time to rest peacefully, and visualize energy circulating up the spine and down the front of the body.

8. The man should withdraw from the woman while still erect, and should not wait until his penis has become flaccid.

The Seven Damages describe the seven conditions under which one should avoid sexual intercourse.

1. If either partner feels genital discomfort or pain.

2. If activity becomes too strenuous.

3. If indulgence has led to weakness.

4. When the man has desire but does not have an erection. Don't force your partner—or yourself. (See also the sixth damage.)

5. When in an overly agitated or anxious emotional state.
6. When the woman does not feel desire, but the man is desperately trying to arouse it. At such times, there is no energy connection.
7. When there is not enough time. In other words, when there is not time for foreplay, or to cultivate emotional response. When one rushes through intercourse, one wastes energy, and undermines the positive effects.

If people can pay attention to these considerations, their sexual activity will enhance their health and their relationship, maintain their youth, and lead to rejuvenation. Otherwise, you may damage your health, shorten your life, or cause other physical problems as well, which may be less severe but just as real.

These ideas seem to emphasize the male point of view—but these activities can help or harm the woman as much as the man. If the male does things well, his partner will benefit as much as he does.

Mutual desire and mutual attraction are more important than mere technique. Sexual activity should not be one-sided. When desire is mutual, benefit is mutual. When desire is one-sided, one side loses. When one side loses, both sides lose.

In reality, it is often not the case that both sides always have the same feeling. This is why cultivation is required to bring both partners to the same point. If both partners cannot come to the same level of interest and attraction, it is best to postpone the lovemaking until feelings are mutual.

Viagra: The Sexual Credit Card

When Pfizer, the giant pharmaceutical company, introduced Viagra in 1998, it created a whirlwind of interest in the medical community—and among men all over the world. It was a huge marketing success.

This drug, and many similar ones that will soon be on the market, can play a role in the treatment of sexual dysfunction, but it has been used in ways that could cause more damage than good. It is often used to try to make up for energy that isn't there, which is like pumping the last bit of oil from a drying well.

We can see, then, that some things that seem to promote sexual ability can actually undermine it—just as the wrong use of credit cards can create a temporary appearance of wealth while actually creating serious financial problems.

Viagra does not really create primal sexual energy: it just helps to expend it. From the point of view of basic natural law, it is like charging purchases on a credit card when you don't have the cash flow to pay for them. But one has to pay for the purchases eventually, and, in a sexual context, one pays by accelerated aging, by the weakening of the kidneys and urogenital system, by stress on the heart, and so on. It is likely that more serious consequences will show up in the future. Furthermore, it is one-sided: the imbalance on the Yang side can lead to imbalances on the Yin side as well.

The best approach, the best kind of aphrodisiac, is a healthy body, balanced emotions, and genuine mutual love. Meditation, qi cultivation, and sensible exercise can all help to improve genuine energy resources.

Guiding Sexual Energy

When people are lonely, they dream about having a lover. Even people who are in a relationship can find themselves frustrated and daydreaming during times when they are apart from each other.

When sexual energy is too abundant, it will often manifest as anxiety, impatience, or irritability. Some people release it through sports, hard work, or physical labor. In Taoist teaching, the energy should be transmuted into qi energy through meditation or Qi Gong, and thus further enhance and rejuvenate one's body. This is sometimes called Inner Alchemy. For a loving couple, there is also a visualization technique that can be used to benefit both partners.

When people are in a relationship, they already have an energetic connection, and also an *information* connection. During times of separation, when they feel a surge of desire, they can lightly visualize the other person, and, very lightly, visualize sending that energy to them. This is not the same as erotic daydreaming: it should not be a sexual fantasy, but an abstract sending of energy.

It is important to emphasize that this technique only works with people who already have a mutual understanding and openness with each other, and who are prepared to receive as well as project. Attempting to use it with (or, more precisely, *on*) someone with whom you do not have an existing relationship, and an understanding about energy sharing, can create far more problems than it can solve. It can lead to a one-sided obsession on your part, and also weaken your energy, since you do not receive any energy in return. All that you get back may be annoyance on the part of the other person.

This technique may seem to be "just imagination," and far too simple to amount to anything. In fact, nature always provides channels for energy to flow; the only question is whether or not the channels are open. This kind of visualization simply opens the gate: in an existing relationship, the channels are already there. In the context of an existing energetic connection, energy wants to flow to the other person to nourish him or her: there is no need to "send" it by using force or effort. The energy will flow where it is directed by a very simple intention, and will continue to flow to complete the circuit, returning transformed to the one who sent it, helping and supporting both partners, and distributing the energy smoothly and peacefully between them.

The Ultimate Romance Pill

Sexuality is a fundamental human desire, shared by all human beings. Regardless of whether one is rich or poor, beautiful or ugly, the nature of the experience and pleasure that it brings is the same. Sex plays very important roles in contributing to and maintaining physical and mental health, in providing energy and motivation. It is crucial for human beings to have an adequate sexual life.

Although there are often religious reasons to abstain from sex, in normal human life, energies can only be balanced through healthy sexual relationship.

Sexual expression is a two-edged sword. It can be a powerful aid in creating a joyful life, but when mishandled it can be very destructive. There are any number of techniques, foods, supplements, medicines, and gadgets devised to enhance sexual experience—but the true basis of sexuality is internal.

Here is the real love potion: take four parts affection, three parts passion, two parts caring, and one part tenderness. Mix the above ingredients with patience and an open heart, and administer with sensitivity and gentleness. Use daily, and you will find that desire will lead to unity and fulfillment.

9

The Miracle of Ordinary Life

To say that romantic relationships are Yin-Yang relationships seems very simple. But if we look closely at the Tai Chi diagram, in which Yin and Yang are divided by a curving line, we can see that the relationship is a dynamic relationship, one that involves constant change and transformation. The fast pace of modern living intensifies this dynamism, leading to even faster rates of change. Maintaining stability in such dynamic relationships is a far greater challenge now than it used to be. There may have been a perfect balance at the time the relationship formed and first stabilized, but things can easily shift out of balance, and people grow apart as quickly as they came together.

As we descend from the higher, abstract level to the concrete, things become exceedingly complicated. Culture, religion, family background, education and profession, and the economy—all these things have an impact on a relationship. These issues have also become intensified in modern life, in which there is far more frequent intercultural contact than ever before.

In spite of all these challenges, the basic patterns of Yin-Yang relationships remain the same. Regardless of the level we are working on, it is important to pay attention to the energy patterns that are behind the surface manifestations. The possible energy patterns themselves are the same at any level of manifestation, and the effective approach to handling them also remains the same.

Many of the differences that exist on the concrete level are sorted out during the process of courtship, before two people fully join together, but challenges always remain. The problem on the concrete level is to bring enough of the abstract clarity into play so that we can untangle some of the complexities of life and see how things that seem chaotic can actually be resolved into a higher order—that is, in terms of energy patterns.

Ultimately, the best ways to deal with things look very simple and mundane, but they are in fact very powerful, because they derive from the inevitable patterns of Yin-Yang relationships. The following points may seem to describe mundane methods or approaches, but thinking about these things can help show how an understanding of Yin-Yang relationships can aid us in dealing with the problems of ordinary life in ways that take advantage of natural, simple, and even inevitable solutions.

Honey, Maybe You're Right

In daily life, anything can become the basis for an argument. Couples can argue about any issue, from household matters to politics, and everyone wants to assert his or her own opinion. But arguments about small matters can accumulate into serious disagreements even, or perhaps especially, when the arguments aren't matters of principle. Over time, this can have serious negative effects on a relationship. Whenever arguments or disputes arise, even if you think you are clearly right, it does no damage to consider the possibility that the other person is right—and to say so. You have nothing to lose. Saying, "Honey, maybe you are right," is one of the most powerful sentences one can say when disagreements arise in a romantic relationship.

Arguments can also be resolved by diversion, which can relieve the heat and personal tension that often goes with disagreements. I once knew an old Chinese couple. The husband was a retired army general. For years, I routinely visited them on Sunday afternoons, and stayed for dinner. This was a very sophisticated couple, and they each had their own well-developed opinions. As they entered their eighties, their memories began to fail, and from time to time they would get into disagreements about various facts. To resolve such arguments, they developed a system: whenever they disagreed about something, they would make a five-dollar bet about it. They would later look up the facts, and find out who had been right. They would each keep their own moneybox for their winnings, and from time to time they would compare their winnings to see whose memory was doing the best, and tease each other about it. In other words, they took what could have been a bad habit and turned it into a game from which they both gained a great deal of pleasure.

If you can take a step back even when you think you are right, you will find that the world in front of you has suddenly become bigger, and you have much more breathing room.

Enjoy the Small Things in Life Now

People have a tendency to look forward to big events, to try to create a big surprise for a partner or lover—a special diamond ring, a surprise vacation overseas, or a special birthday party. This is especially true when we feel we have done something in the past for which we need to be forgiven. In real life, though, when today is gone it is gone for good. It cannot be brought back. Tomorrow's joy does not make up for yesterday's sorrow.

It is better to live in the present. A small joy today is here now, not in the theoretical future. A simple walk in the park can mean more than a future vacation. In our lives, most memorable events are usually not "big" events, such as graduations, weddings, and so on; they are "small" things: playing in the snow on a remarkable Christmas Eve, a particularly pleasant dinner, an unplanned conversation that somehow meant more than any rehearsed speech or elaborate ceremony.

The joys in life and love are strung on a chain of small events, not giant hoops.

Avoid Saying, "How Many Times Do I Have to . . ."

This is one of the most common remarks made by someone who has a complaint. This phrase does not really have much power—except perhaps the power to irritate.

Why is it so hard for people to hear your message? It may be because they have heard it before, and they have already decided what to do about it—which means, often enough, that they have decided not to do anything about it.

Sometimes, of course, it is just an expression of exasperation, and there is no intention of actually affecting the other person, but if we really want the other person to hear and respond, we have to ask ourselves what it is about the message that keeps it from getting through.

As we have pointed out before, everything manifests from inner to outer. When you find yourself in such a situation, examine yourself first. What is really going on inside of you? Without some understanding of the inner situation, this kind of remark will simply continue to appear, and continue to be ineffective.

Play the "Opposite" Role

The "opposite" role can be the supporting role. While generally one person is Yang and the other is Yin in a partnership, in daily life there is a good deal of variability in who plays which role. When your partner is Yang, you play Yin, and vice versa. Yang and Yin complement each other: Yin and Yin do not, nor do Yang and Yang.

When one person is distressed, the other should be supporting; when one is aggressive, the other should be yielding, until the opportunity arises to take the aggressive role; when one is very overexcited or too optimistic, the other should be calm and cautious.

Get Out of Your Routine

During courtship, or the beginning of a relationship, life tends to be full of sparks and wonder: concerts, dances, parties, hiking, philosophical conversations, poetry, romantic dinners, and so on. There are always new things, and there are always changing rhythms. But as relationships endure and become stabilized, everything becomes routine: grocery shopping, laundry, car maintenance, driving the kids, and so on. Romance is gone: everything focuses on the TV, on work, and on the children. People often complain about being "tied and tired," but everyone seems to be stuck with it. Life becomes boring and tiresome; the relationship loses excitement and wonder.

Learn to get out of the routine of daily life from time to time. Once in a while, do something spontaneous or "crazy." When water is stirred up, the air bubbles enhance the oxygen level of the water and make it better for supporting life. Learn to change old patterns. Go out for a special dinner for no special reason. Buy a bouquet without waiting for a "special" event. Small surprises are often better than bigger fulfillments that are already expected.

Use these small surprises and changes of rhythms as ways to fall in love again.

Find Times To Be Apart

There is a saying that a reunion after a short absence is often better than a new marriage. A long separation might kill a relationship, but a short separation can enhance romance. It is human nature to take for granted what we already have. We lose our sense of appreciation. This is especially true for a couple that lives together for a long time. They come to count on mutual support and advice, and do not realize how special these "ordinary" things are.

If a couple occasionally spends time apart, they will be reminded of the value of what they have had all along. If the wife goes to visit her family for a while, it's true that the husband might find a sense of freedom for the first few days. Then he will gradually find that there are holes in his day, and things that need to be done that he seldom has to do for himself.

Appreciate Differences

Men and women may be equal, but they are not the same. Do not expect your partner to act, think, or respond the way you do. We must realize that because men manifest Yang energy and women manifest Yin energy, they are naturally different.

Women may seem illogical to men; men may seem mechanical to women, especially when they are in a romantic relationship. (This kind of difference doesn't seem to exist in the same way when it comes to work relationships.) A surprise bouquet might make a woman happy for days, but if a woman gives a man a special gift, he might just say "Thanks," put it down, and go back to watching TV.

A woman might ask a man to do something, and go on in some detail about it; the man might just want to get on with it and get it done. He might think the talking is beside the point; for her, the conversation might be the reason why the request was important in the first place. Women are more focused on the process; men on the result.

There is a reason why men and women are different. Without this difference, there would be no polarity. Without polarity, there would be no attraction. Without attraction, there would be no relationship.

If men and women were the same, life would be very boring. This is why you should not expect your partner or lover to always respond the way you do. Learn to accept and appreciate difference, and play with it. Learn to understand the value of difference.

Appreciate Imperfections

Besides the natural differences between men and women, there is also the issue of the imperfections that every person has.

Many people keep certain bad habits or flaws throughout their lives. Spending one's life with such a person can provide guaranteed annoyance for as long as the relationship lasts.

As long as these traits don't involve fundamental principles, it may be better to learn to accept them, to say, "You know, that's just the way this person is." This simple switch in our way of thinking can resolve a lot of problems.

A perfect person, without any bad habits or flaws, might be very boring to be with. In addition, if you found someone who was completely perfect, it would probably turn out that you were not perfect to that person!

If your partner nags you, try to relax and enjoy the nagging. Think of the nagging as a special form of attention. If you didn't matter, would your partner spend the time and energy it takes to nag you?

Seal Small Cracks As Soon As Possible

Regardless of how compatible two people are, by living together there will inevitably be friction between them. Resolve small differences as soon as they appear. Patch small cracks—don't let them become big splits. If small cracks become big splits, and then become a series of fissures, they can be very hard to patch without leaving traces, and without compromising the structure of the relationship.

A skillful gardener attends to weeds as soon as they appear. If weeds are allowed to grow for too long, getting rid of them may disrupt the garden.

Never underestimate the impact of small problems. Be sensitive to small things, and you will keep them from becoming big ones.

Don't Let Hope Disappoint You

Fulfillment or disappointment comes from expectations. We measure what we have against what we expected to have. The less you expect, the less disappointment you will have, and the more fulfilled you will be. This is a general rule for life—and for relationships.

Do not expect more than what your partner can offer. Accept each other's limitations. No matter how great a relationship is, your life is larger than the relationship. The world is bigger than the two of you. Do not expect that you will have complete fulfillment and happiness just through a romantic relationship. It will always be necessary to have supportive, nonromantic friends as well as a romantic partner; there are things one can say to a friend more readily than to a lover.

Sometimes energies accumulate in us that need to be manifested, but these energies cannot be manifested in a romantic context; it is often necessary to find a channel for release outside of our romantic relationship.

The previous points may seem very ordinary, and even banal. But remember the key idea: the best way is the natural way; the natural way is the simple way; and the simple way is often the ordinary way. People always hope for some special, magical techniques that will make their lives special, as special as they secretly feel they really are, or really should be. This is because we have forgotten how special, how precious, our actual lives are. We think we can make them more special by turning the volume louder, by adding extra tracks on the recording, bringing in wawa pedals and electric organs with all sorts of unusual built-in synthetic effects.

But it's just the opposite. As the Taoist classics say, it is the five colors that dim the vision, and the five flavors that numb the tongue. It is, in other words, the addiction to increasingly stronger stimulation that makes us unable to feel what is already there. If we can stop, turn down the amplification, and pay real attention, we can find out that what is simple and ordinary has more depth than any layers of paint we can slap on it, no matter how colorful the paint may make it seem.

We all want special solutions, since needing a special solution confirms that we are special people. But in fact, our problems are solved not by imitating other people's solutions; they are solved by seeing our own problems clearly and doing something about them. Much of the "machinery" of meditation training exists only to bring us to this point; the same thing is true of Feng Shui. As a famous psychiatrist once said, the point of psychotherapy is often just to get to the point where there are finally two people in a room who are able to carry on a conversation. The point of Feng Shui Theory, of Yin-Yang Theory, and of Five Element Theory is to bring us to the point where we are able to be in a place and be aware of how we experience it, and to be with others and experience them as being in the same place as us. It is very simple, very ordinary, and that is why it is very special.

10

The Eternal Transformation

Love, and loving relationships, at every level and scale, pervade our lives. Love plays a key role in transforming us, and all beings, to a higher level. This does not mean that there is a fixed target or a set goal to this transformation: each person, each being, has an individual path of transformation over the course of his or her existence. The important thing is the process itself.

If each life is its own process of transformation, does this tell us anything about the meaning of life? As far back as we know, people have been seeking the answer to this question. The ancient sages answered this question by saying that the purpose of living is to enhance the well-being of all living things. The meaning of life is to contribute to the continuation of life in the universe.

This sacred question can also be seen as a misguided question, *since the purpose of living is simply living itself; the meaning of life is life itself.* In other words, the purpose of living is simply to live as fully as possible. Living one's life in a way that tries to make it fit into a concept of what it means, or what it should be, is to limit what one's life can be, and to undermine the possibility of encountering its deepest meaning. This does not mean that it is wrong or useless to have plans—just that it is self-defeating to try to force one's life to fit completely into the box of one idea about what it can be. Many things in life are beyond control. If one takes the attitude that to be meaningful one's life must fit some preconceived notion, as soon as something happens that doesn't fit, one will have the feeling that one's whole life has been derailed. Some people sit for years brooding about what they think of as a train wreck, but people with a less rigid point of view would recognize it as the opening of new, unexpected possibilities.

We have been talking about love and romantic relationships throughout this book. Now it is time to revisit the question "What is love?" Many people think that by defining love, we lose the essence of love. This is true in some way on an individual level, since the manifestations of love are so different that it would be hard for any definition based on one example to fit all. But when seen from a higher level, there is a common force and pattern behind all the manifestations. *Love is the process and state of the dynamic balance of Yin and Yang*. This can be played out within one person, from one person to another, mutually between two people, or among all living things.

Many people try to define love from an idealistic point of view, in terms of such things as giving and self-sacrifice, or unconditional love. From the point of view of Yin-Yang Theory, however, no one-way street can be regarded as whole or complete. Simple, unconditional love that does not look for any return actually does have a condition: the giving and the reward take place simultaneously, within the same person. This is why a return from an external source is not required. The love parents feel for their children may seem unconditional, but parents enjoy the caring and loving, and receive their return from that activity.

And so we begin our discussion of love with self-love, the balance of Yin and Yang within oneself that makes one self-fulfilled and self-contained. Many people think of being "self-contained" as being self-sufficient in the sense of being unrelated to anything outside oneself—of being cut off and comfortable with being cut off. This is the opposite of what we mean. To be self-fulfilled and self-contained as a result of establishing an inner harmony is the *necessary basis* of harmonious relationships between oneself and others. No real harmonious relationship with others can exist if one is in a state of inner chaos and discord. When we achieve inner harmony, we can love others. Any loving relationship should be balanced: it should not be a matter of sacrificing or simply hoping for a response. Balance should be innate in the relationship, rather than being something negotiated by acts of sacrifice and payment. When the balance is spontaneous and simultaneous, love is truly itself; when balance is negotiated and bartered, the relationship is closer to business than to love.

As the circle of love—the scale of the Tai Chi—expands, the presence of immediate, simultaneous harmony also expands: from internal harmony to harmony between two entities—and to larger levels of harmony as well. When two people are in a harmonious relationship, their relationship can then exist in harmony with their family, and in a larger circle with society as a whole. Each expansion of the circle of harmony is an increase in the depth of love. This is why a relationship that only includes the couple may be more superficial, and shorter lasting, than one that includes broader circles of family, friends, and community. From the individual to the larger society, each level has its own Yin-Yang balance. The more levels that come into balance in a loving relationship, the more depth that relationship has.

For human beings, the union of Yin and Yang energy in loving relationships occurs in the context of seeking happiness, security, fulfillment, and comfort. Yet in all unions, in all relationships, joy is always accompanied by sorrow; fulfillment is always accompanied by disappointment. In different unions, these are mingled in different proportions. People often say that marriage or other committed relationships are like a wall: those who are inside want to get out; those who are outside want to get in. Is the Creator playing games with us? Why are we trapped in this sort of contradictory situation?

Maybe we need to look at the human situation, and male and female relationships, from a higher point of view. Some couples maintain a single happy relationship for a lifetime; there are people who struggle through many short relationships. Is the former any better than the latter? Is one more fortunate than the other? If a person has an easy and happy life, it may be seen as a blessing. And yet, it may also be that the person is just taking a break in this lifetime, and is not yet ready for a higher level of challenge. Some people may go through many difficult episodes and tragic relationships; others might think of this as disastrous, but it could be that these people are ready for more vigorous training and more difficult lessons.

Loving relationships, married life: these are vehicles that move us through the process of eternity. There may be fulfillment or a lack of it; there may be a temporary union or a lifelong marriage: these are simply manifestations of the process. What we need to appreciate is that we have a life, and we need to move through the process of living while maintaining an awareness of ourselves in this process.

Life is both ordinary and special. We seem to come to our particular lives almost by accident. Although there is always destiny, the fact that in the vastness of time and space one life meets and becomes linked to another is so unlikely that it is almost like magic.

Enjoyment, achievements, arguments, divorce: all these are external manifestations that we judge from our attachments. This is the Yang aspect of things.

What is as important, or even more important, is the Yin aspect—the inner transformation that occurs in the midst of all these outer events. This inner transformation is a matter of what we are becoming.

Toward Spirituality

The union of love is a spiritual process, a process of transformation to a higher level of existence. But what does it mean to call this process spiritual? How are we defining what is spiritual?

Religious people tend to define spirituality in terms of faith and religion. Philosophers may approach it slightly differently, in terms of moral values and social behavior. People ordinarily tend to think of spirituality as a matter of morality, good behavior, and good-heartedness. All these definitions are incomplete. People with sincere good hearts may not have enough wisdom to act well. Morality is often shaped by the culture and the times: something that was regarded as immoral centuries ago might be regarded as virtuous now; what is seen as abnormal in one culture might be seen as normal in another. Spirituality cannot be simply a matter of religion or culture, which are relative and changeable phenomena.

Our judgment of things or people, and our consequent behavior, makes us seem good or bad, moral or immoral, generous or stingy, compassionate or cold, loving or cruel. But this has to do with the breadth of our vision. Things look very different from a narrower or from a broader point of view, and the ultimate basis of the narrower or more limited perspective is the limitation imposed by time and space. *Spirituality has to do with the scale of perception of time and space.* If one perceives time and space from a larger scale, one naturally tends to be more spiritual.

For example, if a young man gets fired from a job, he may be disappointed, frustrated, or even angry with the boss who fired him. A few months later, if he finds a better job, his animosity toward the previous boss may dissipate, and they may even come to get along. A few years later, if he becomes very successful and fulfilled in his new job, he may even be thankful to the previous boss who fired him. The response to the same event can change from very negative to very positive as time unfolds.

If from the very beginning one can see things from a greater perspective, one's reactions will be different—and so will one's behavior. At the moment of being fired, a young man might realize that the job was not for him, and feel set free to search for a better opportunity. He might just smile and say a pleasant goodbye to the boss who fired him. Similarly, if a relationship falls apart, and one can see the larger pattern as this starts to happen, it may be possible to get beyond the initial bitterness and pain, and move more directly into the stage of a newer and larger life. We often hear people say that their partner is their whole life, and that if the relationship ever fell apart, life would be over. But if the relationship does fall apart, after a period of initial distress and bitterness the person's life is often transformed: energy that was locked up is released, and a new life opens up. A broken heart is not necessarily the end of the road: it may be the beginning.

If we live in a confined space, we can see only a limited picture. If we stand close to a building, we may see only the door and a part of the facade; we may have no way to appreciate the building as a whole. If we stand a hundred feet away and get a larger view, we can get a more complete impression of the whole building. If we stand even farther back, we can see not only the building, but also the neighborhood and surroundings. This will give us an even more complete view. The bigger the perspective, the more complete the picture.

In the same way, if we stand very close to people, we see that one may be better looking than others; we have clear opinions, and definite judgments. But if we stand five hundred feet away, we cannot tell one person from another: there is no differentiation, and no judgment.

When astronauts went into space and saw how minute the earth was, they could not help feeling a greater sense of humility. The greater the vision of time and space we have, the humbler we become, the less we judge things in terms of transitory, surface manifestations, and the more compassionately we see things.

The scale on which one experiences time and space can be seen as a measure of spirituality. Many people are focused on what is nearby: job, family, children, and house. They resonate with the joys and sorrows of family and friends. What is more distant is less real and less important. The news of distant joys and catastrophes seems like vague rumors; a hundred thousand deaths are "just a number." The sympathies of highly spiritual people extend further. For very holy people, sympathy and compassion extend throughout the world, to all beings, not just in the present, but also from the past through the future.

Another name for the process of broadening or enlarging our perspective is "transcendence." The biggest obstacle to transcendence is attachment. Attachment is the source of human suffering. Attachment derives from ignorance: the inability to see things in their true nature. A larger perspective allows us to see things in terms of their whole form, rather than their partial form. When we live in terms of a bigger scale of time and space, we naturally come to realize that what we try so hard to grab and hold on to is in fact transitory; and so it is easier to let go. In this way, our attitude becomes more spiritual.

If love is a spiritual process, we need to approach relationships from a higher point of view, from the perspective of a greater expanse of time and space. We do need to live from moment to moment, but we cannot lose sight of the larger scale. We cannot hang on for too long to transient or minor events of daily life. If we see the events of the moment from a larger perspective, they do not seem as pressing, or as all-important, as they might seem if our viewpoint is limited to the moment.

We know that life is more than a biological process. We need to realize that life is also more than an emotional process. *The process of living is a spiritual process.* We should not create illusions for ourselves, and end up trapped in one particular moment. Yet, though each moment is transitory, it is also real, and precious—no matter how it manifests. Whether it is good or bad, we need to be thankful for having the opportunity to experience it. Fun, laughter, joy, and happiness are all wonderful—and transitory. Furthermore, without the contrast of pain and sorrow they are shallow: only difficulties can provide depth.

Only people who have experienced setbacks and failure in life can fully appreciate what life is. Only people who have experienced loss in a romantic relationship can have a deep appreciation of what love is. No life, no relationship, can be all negative or all positive. All experiences are transitory, and it is the movement between what we think of as positive and negative that gives us depth and energy. When we can see these transformations from a larger point of view, we can stop grasping after one extreme and running from the other, and thus we can begin to gain a sense of inner balance and peace. Only inner peace, if we can find it in the process of living and loving, is eternal.

What is this inner peace? It is not a static, unchanging state. Rather, it is a constant awareness of and participation in the interactions, the unions and separations, between Yin and Yang at each level of experience. It is the realization that, no matter what, all experience is built out of these loving interactions, and that no matter what the quality of any immediate event, it is part of a larger story—and that the larger story is, ultimately, a love story.

Index

Y